Copyright © 2018 by Paul Shore

All rights reserved. No part of this publication may be reproduced, distributed, or transmitted in any form or by any means, including photocopying, recording, or other electronic or mechanical methods, without the prior written permission of the publisher, except in the case of brief quotations embodied in critical reviews and certain other noncommercial uses permitted by copyright law. For permission requests, write to the publisher, through our various social media channels.

Dear Colorist,

We would like to appreciate you for purchasing this coloring book. Thanks for being a part of our dreams and we welcome you to our wonderful community. We hope you find total satisfaction coloring your favorite pages in this book.

We have a **pleasant gift** wrapped up on our home page for you. Go to https://paulshorebooks.com to receive your gift by subscribing to our mailing list.

Also, you will have access to a **free digital version** of this coloring book. Watch out for this towards the end ☺

Once again thanks for supporting our work by purchasing this coloring book publication. Now pick up your favorite coloring tool, sit back, relax and let that artistic spark shine forth.

Paul Shore and Team.

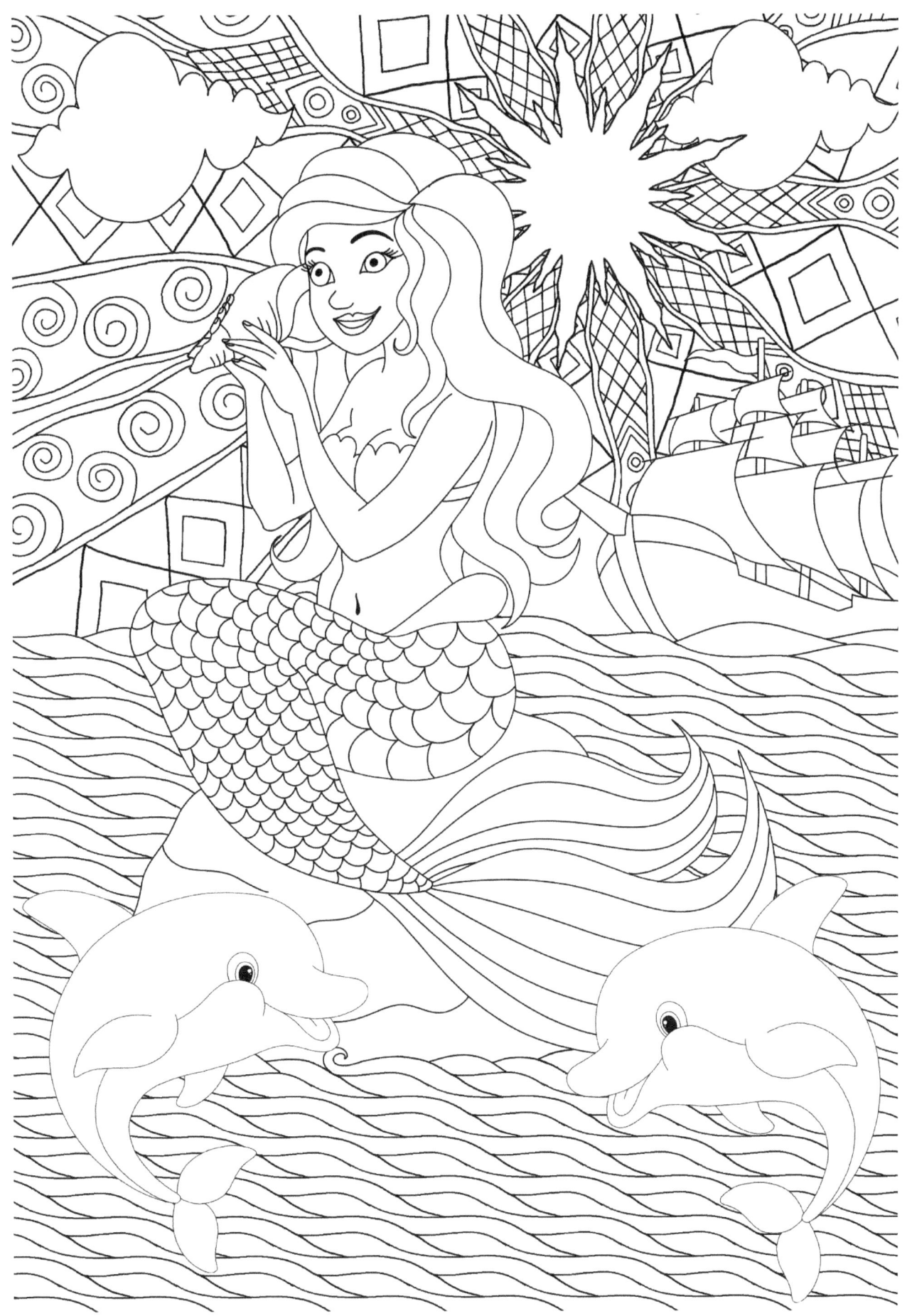

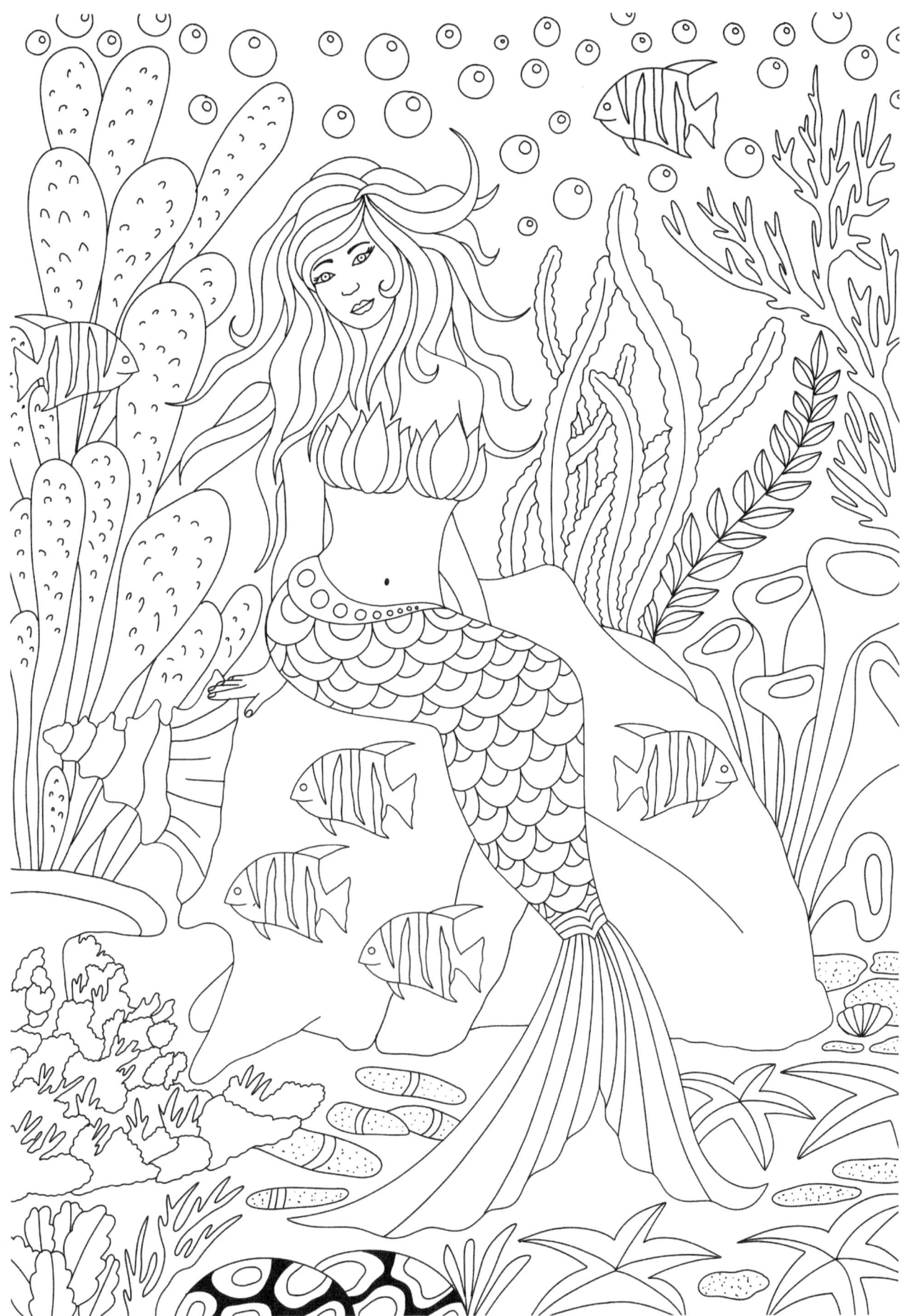

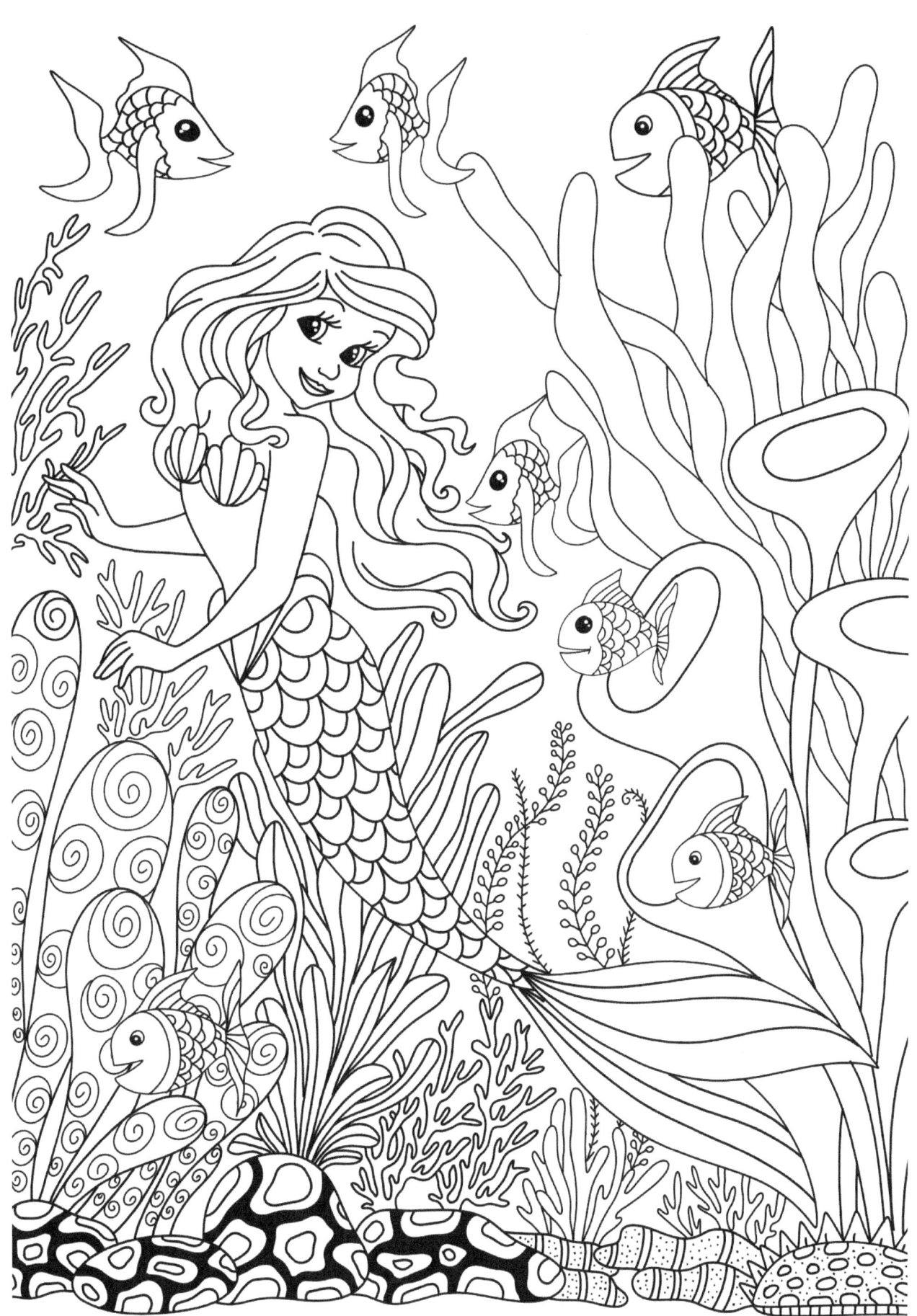

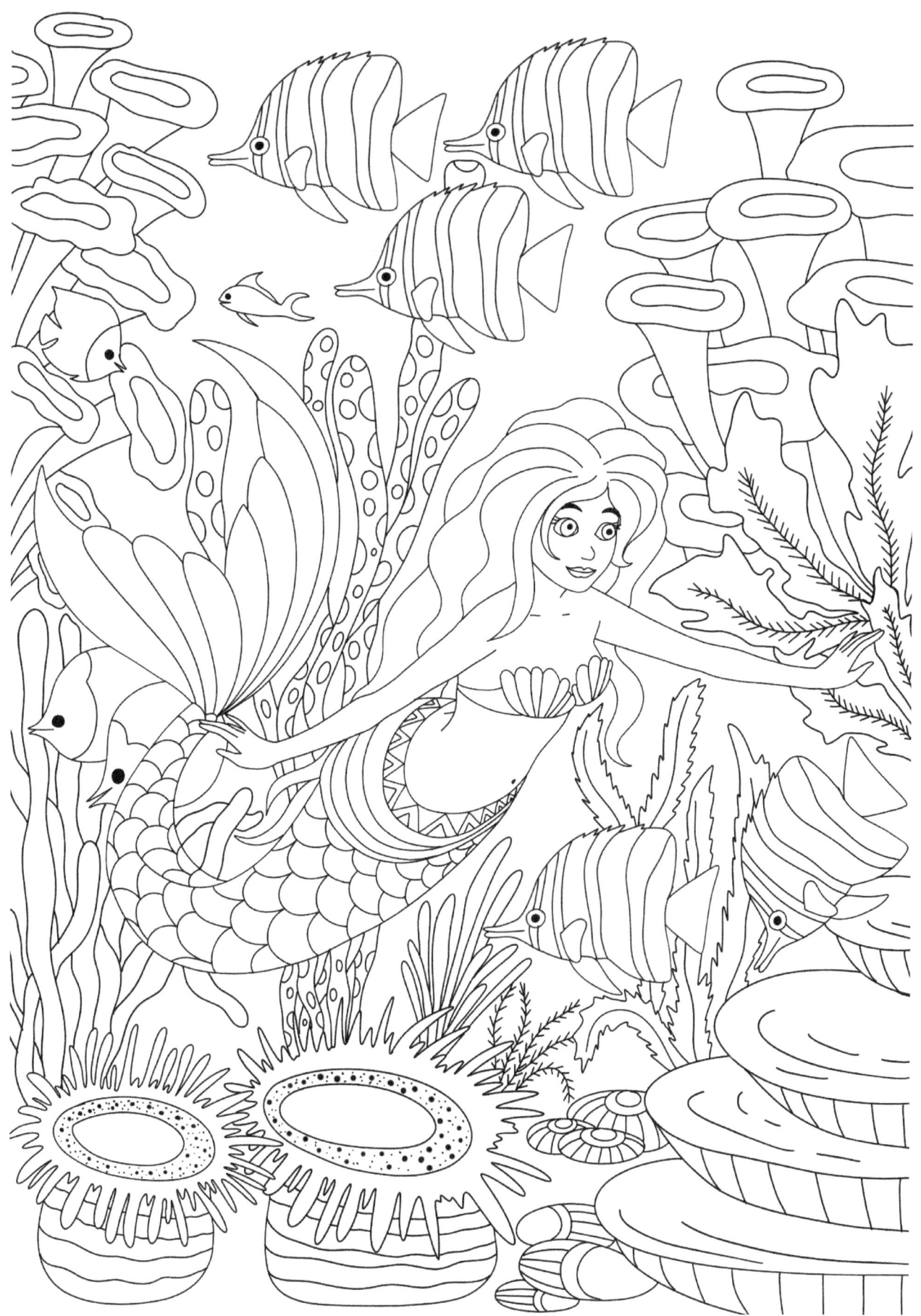

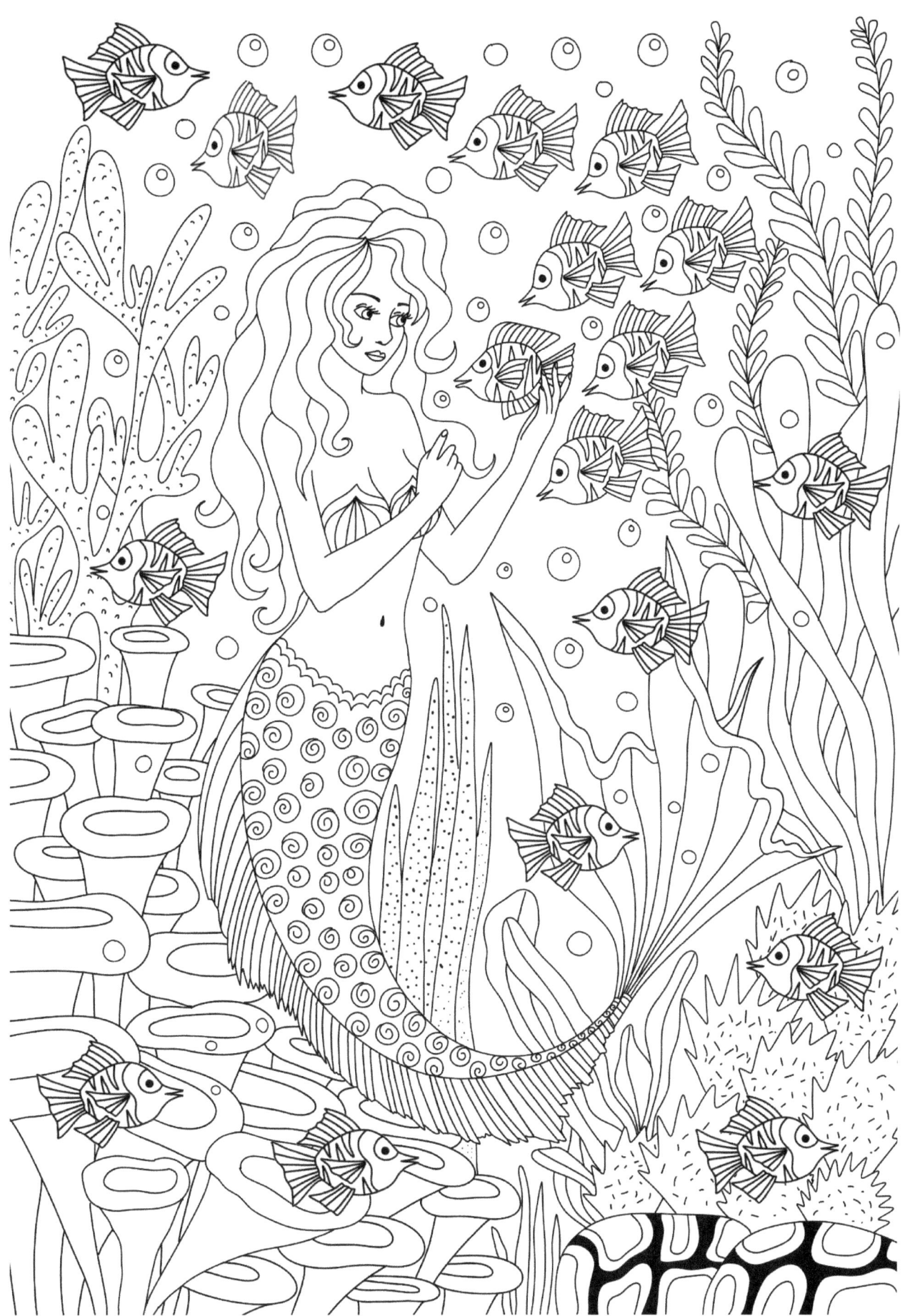

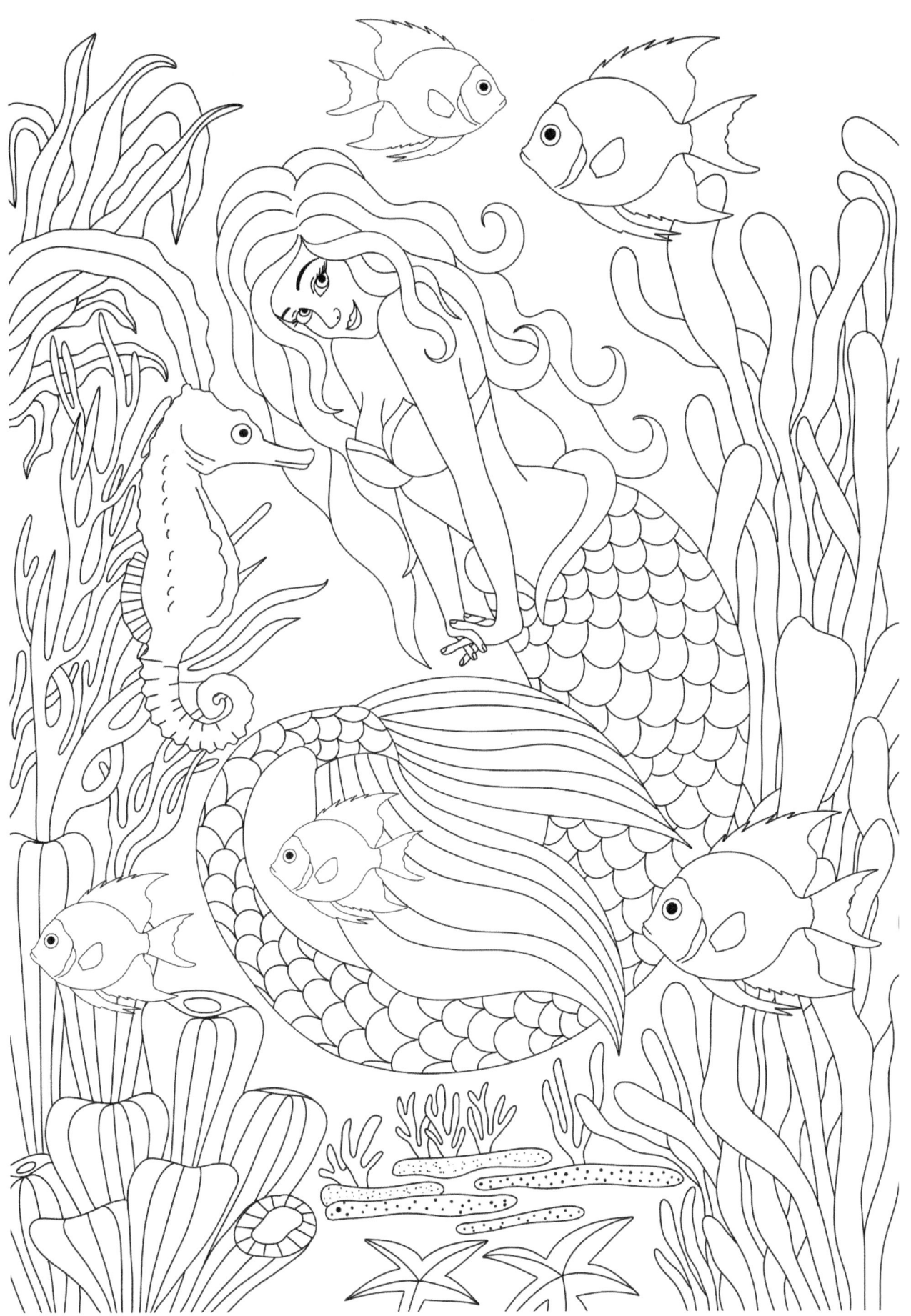

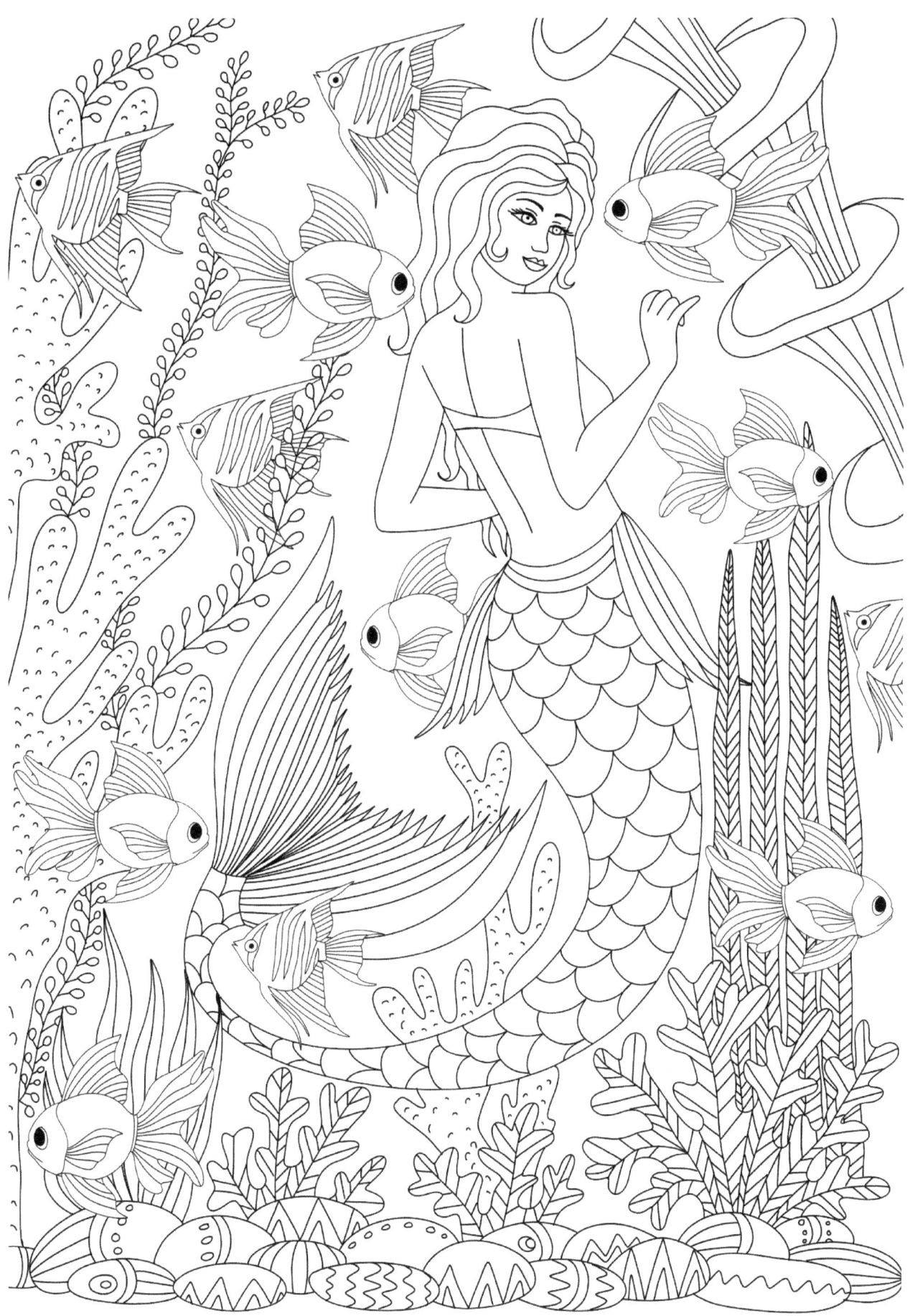

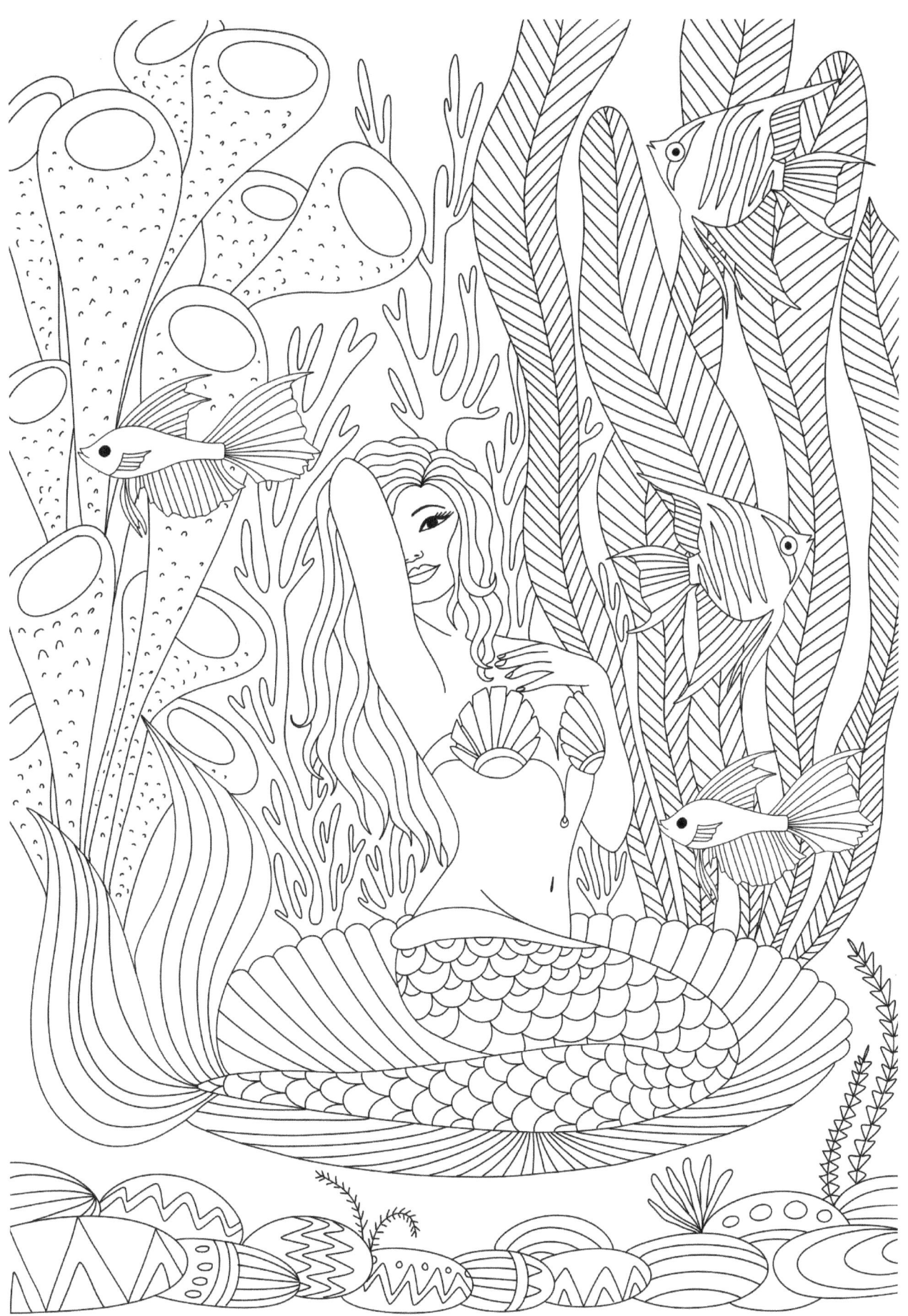

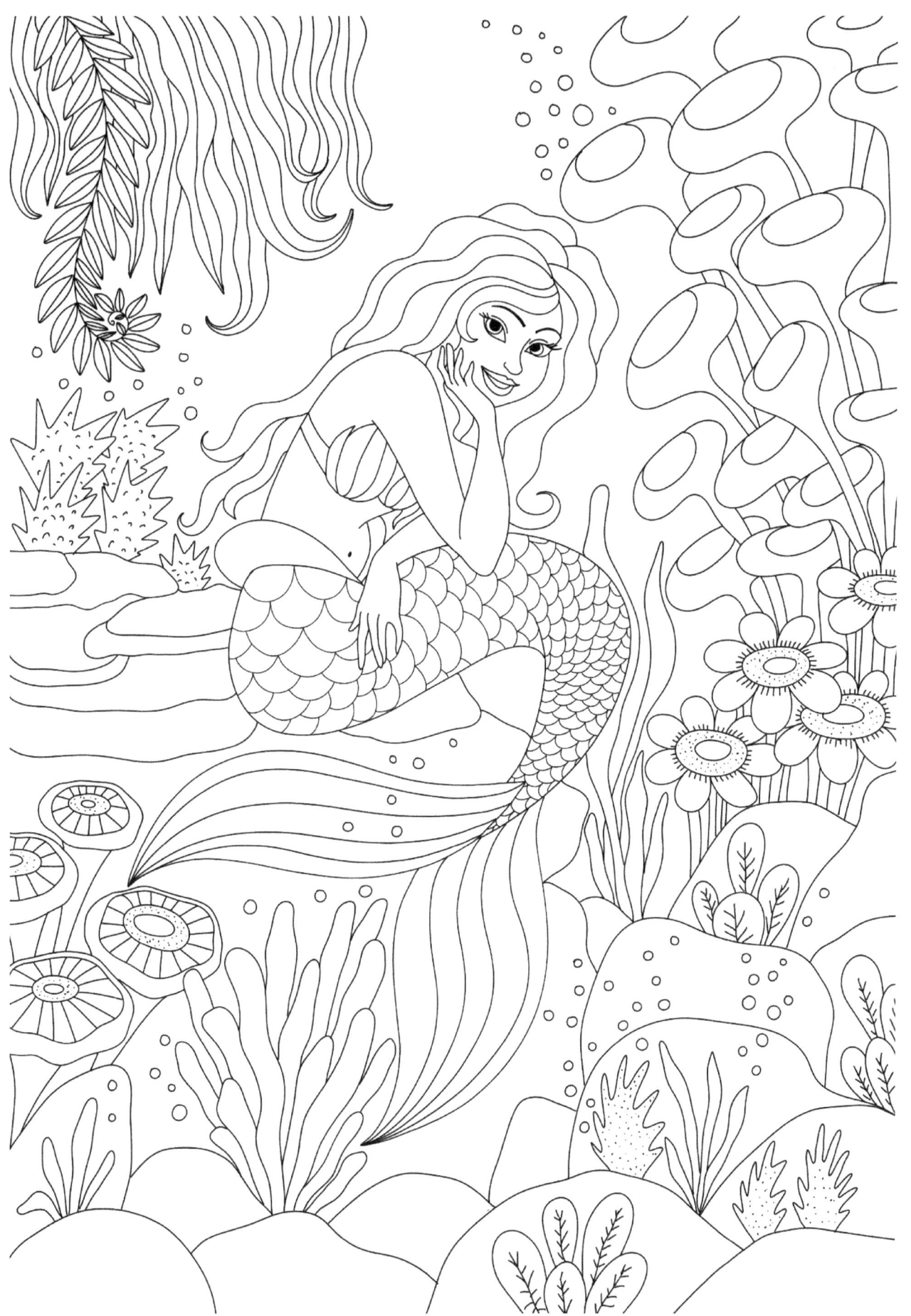

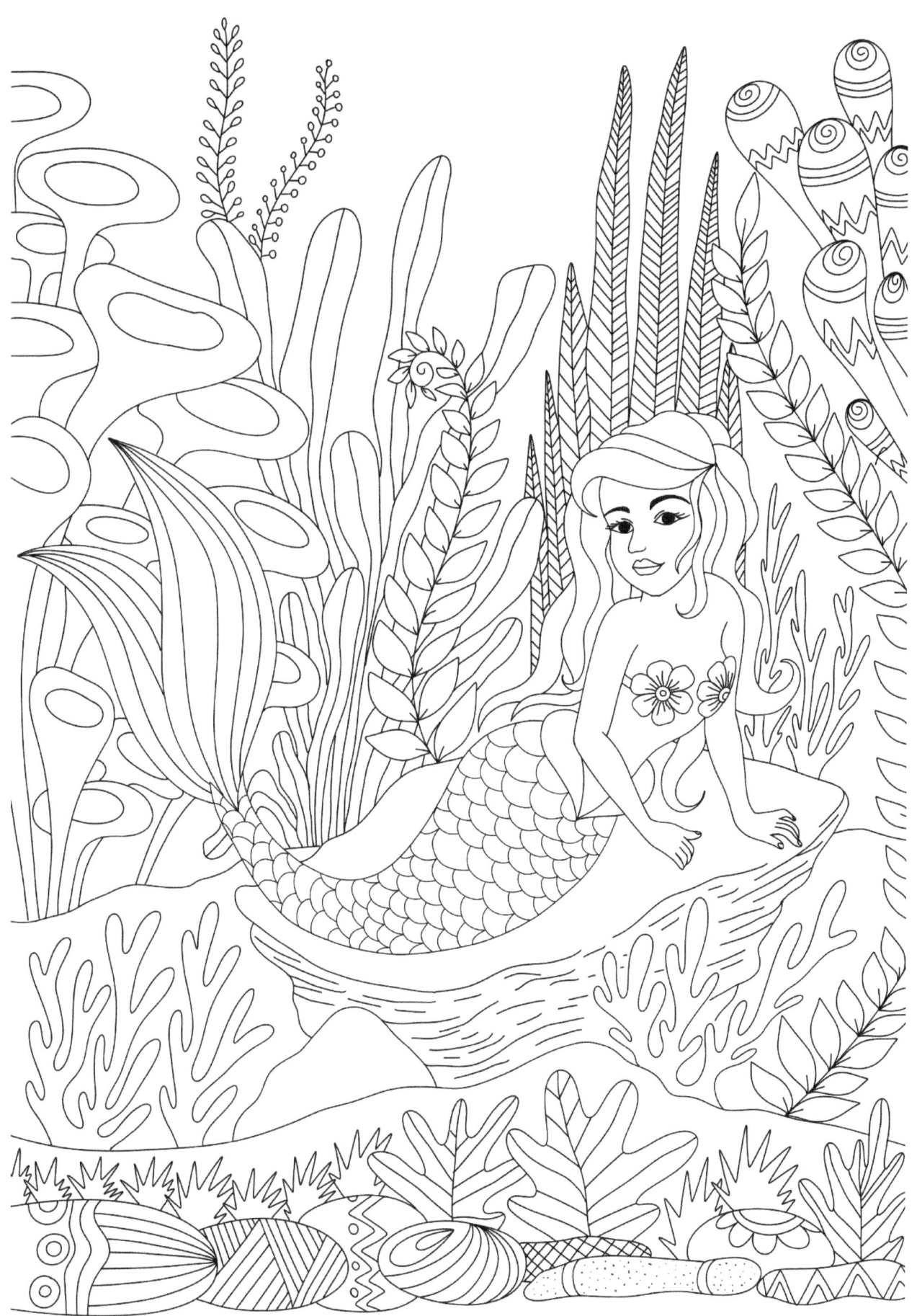

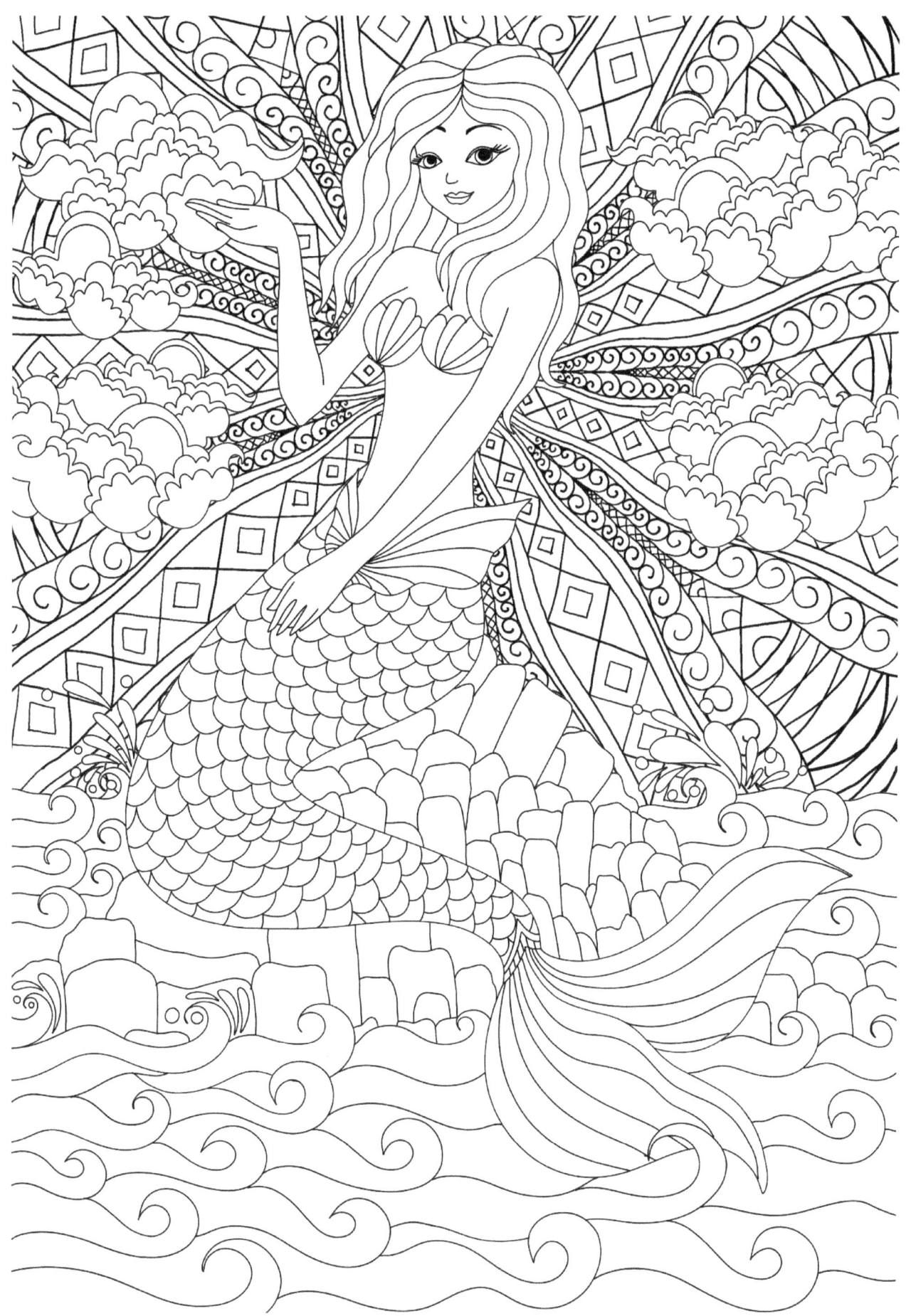

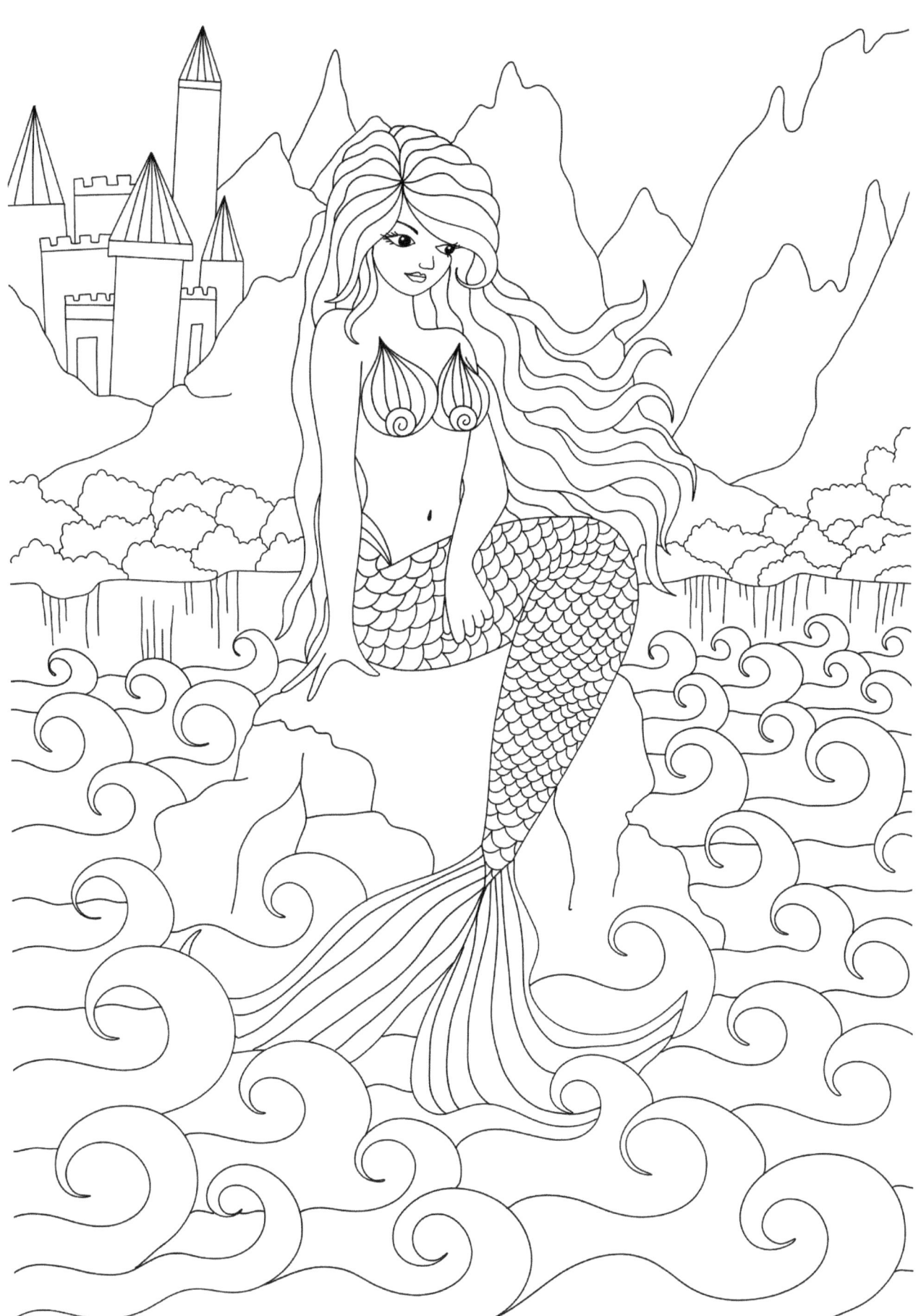

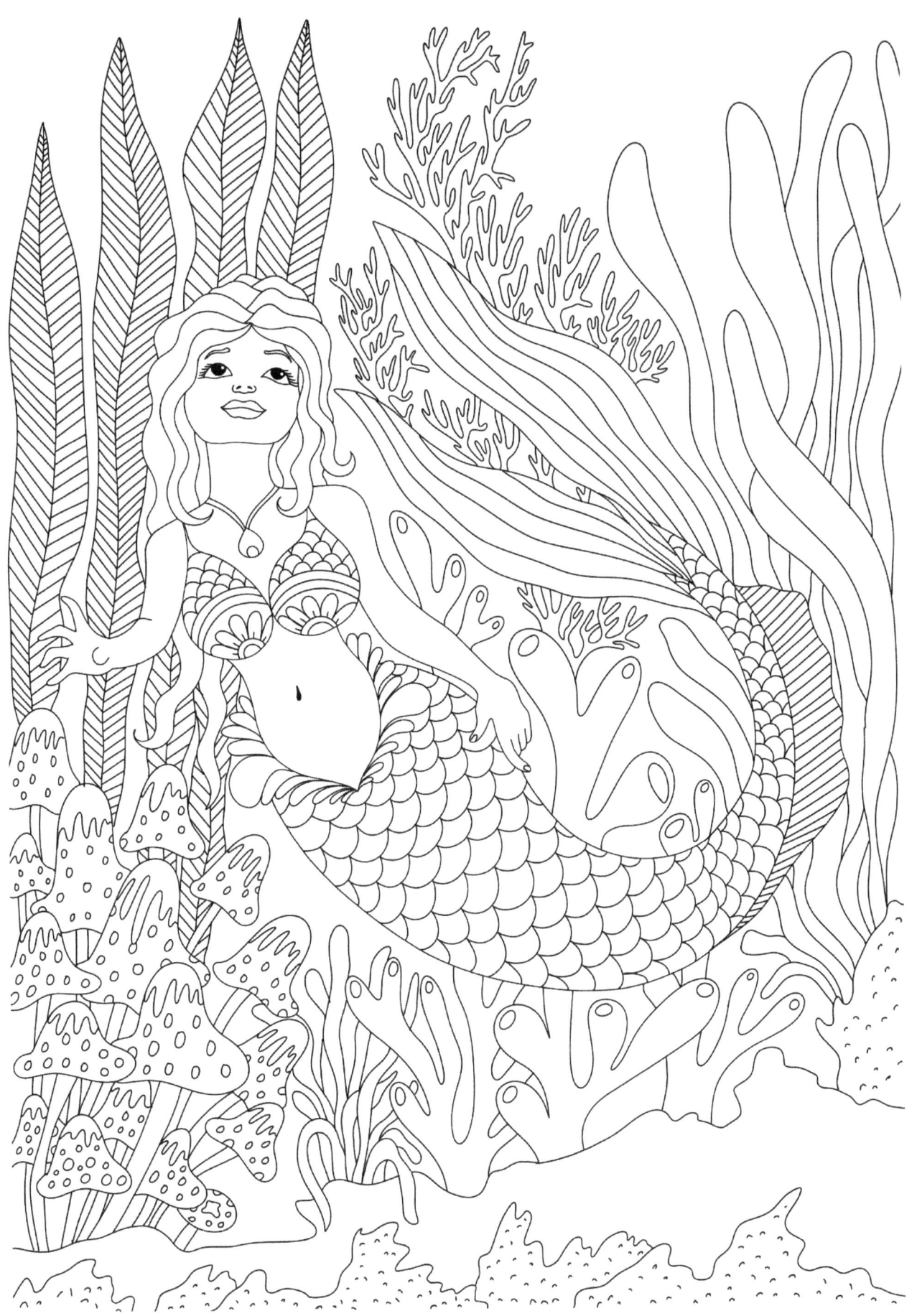

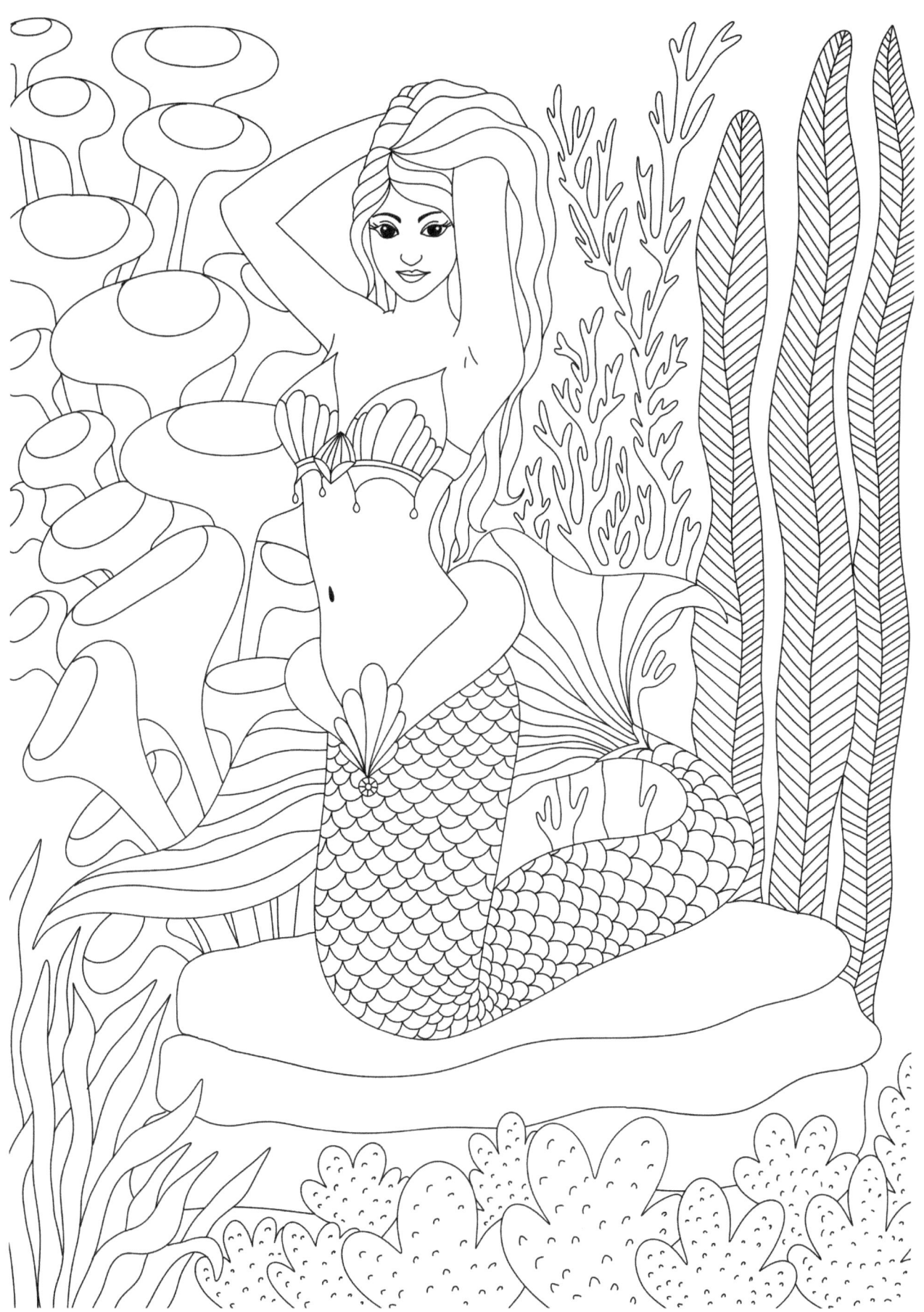

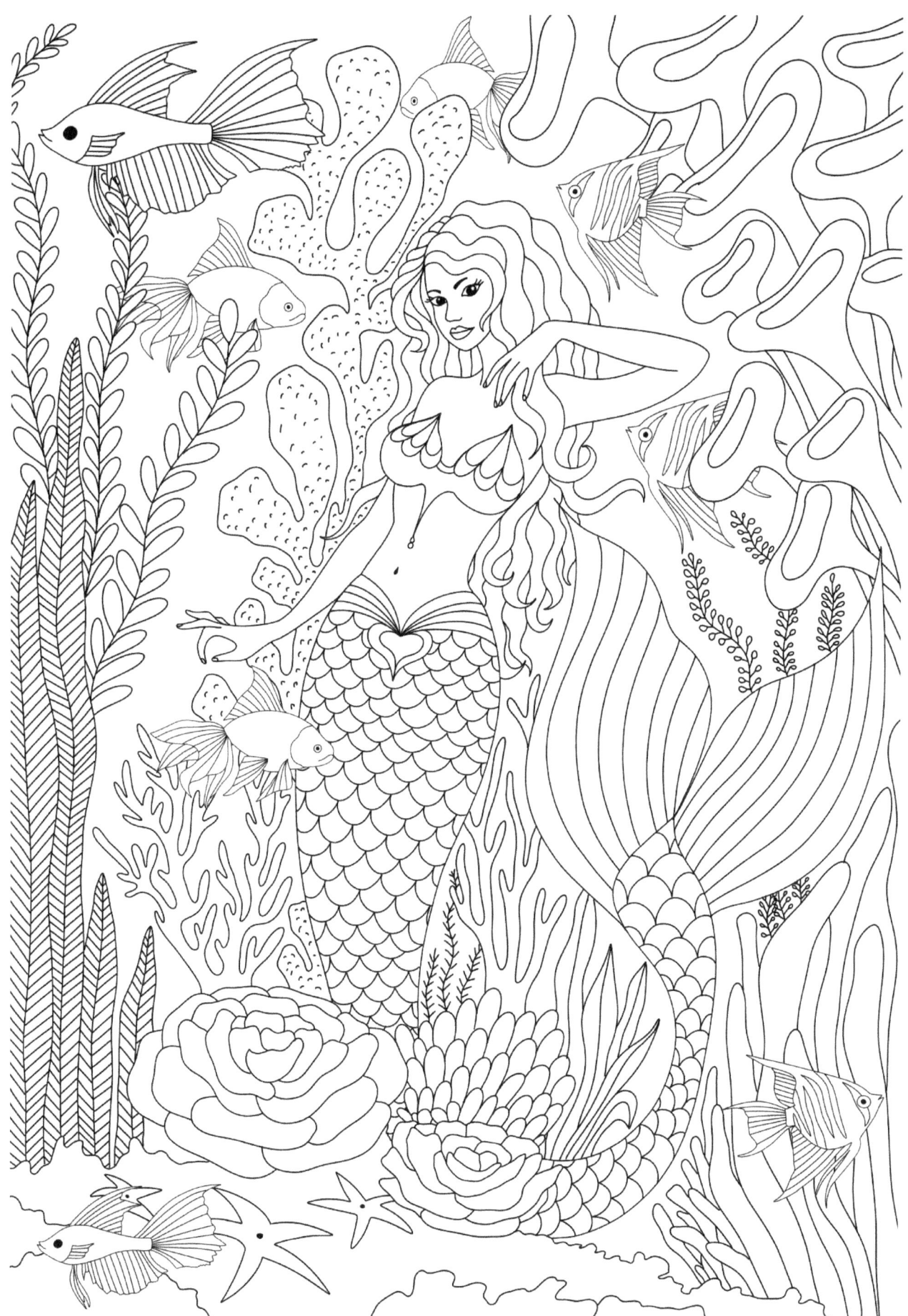

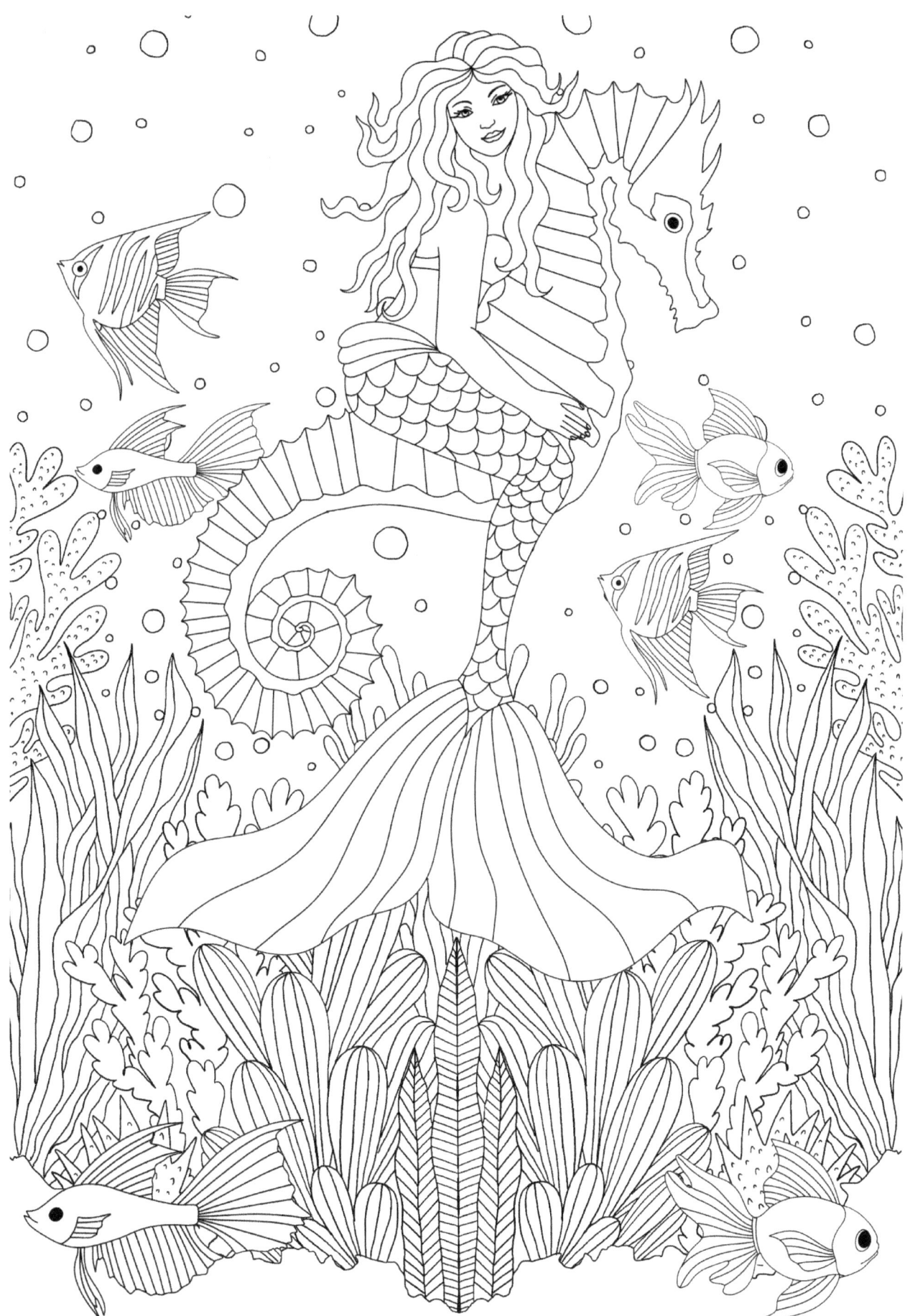

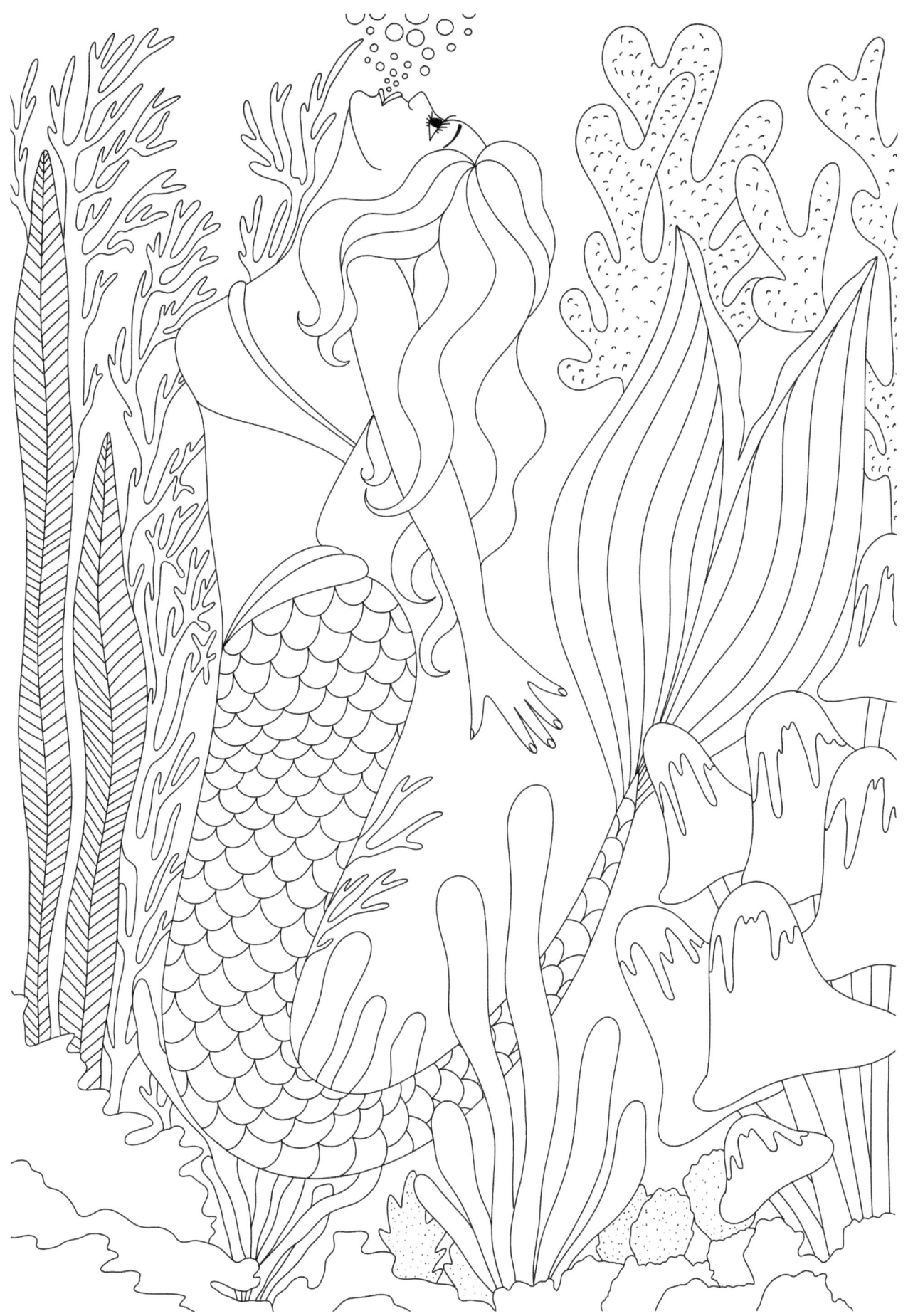

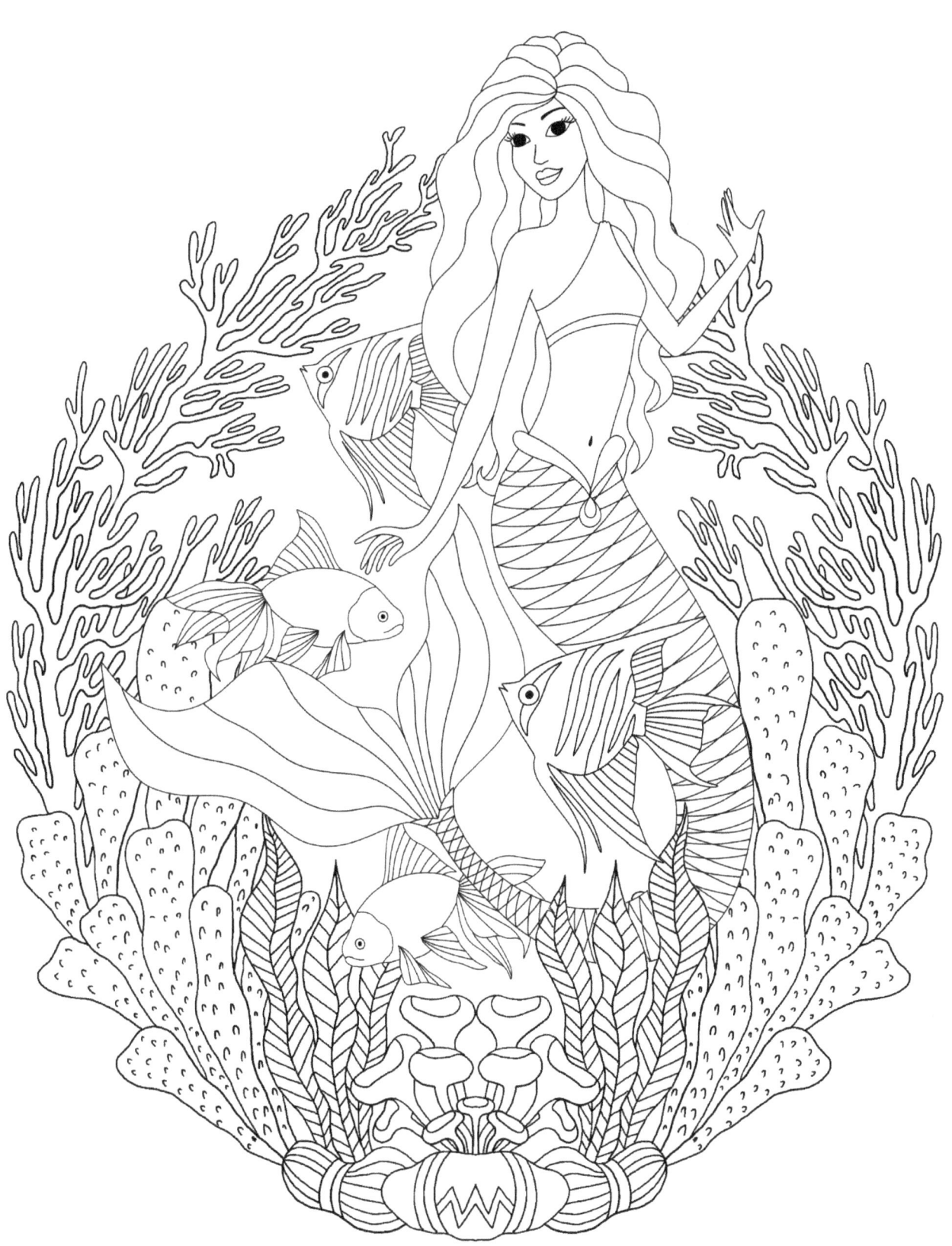

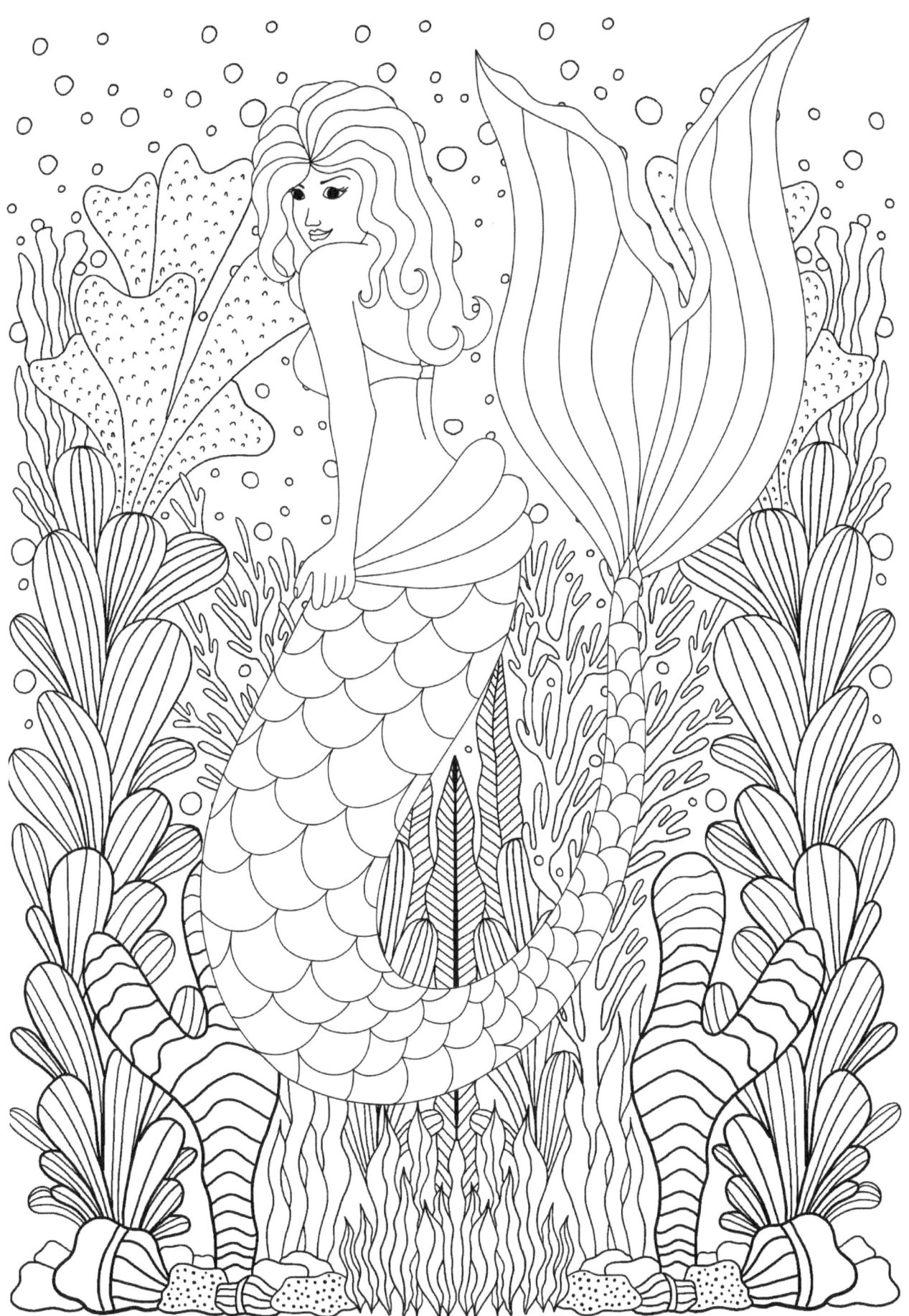

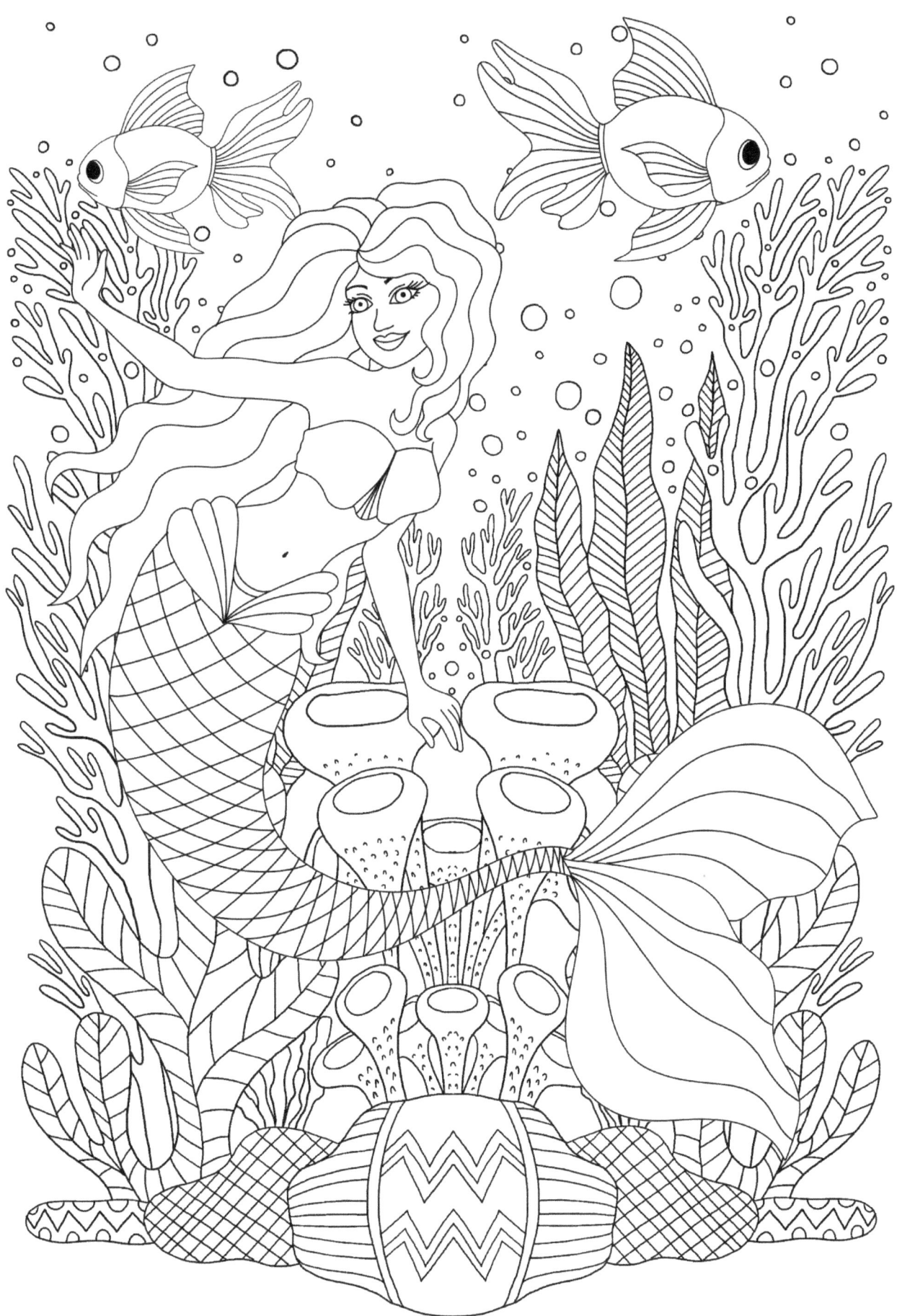

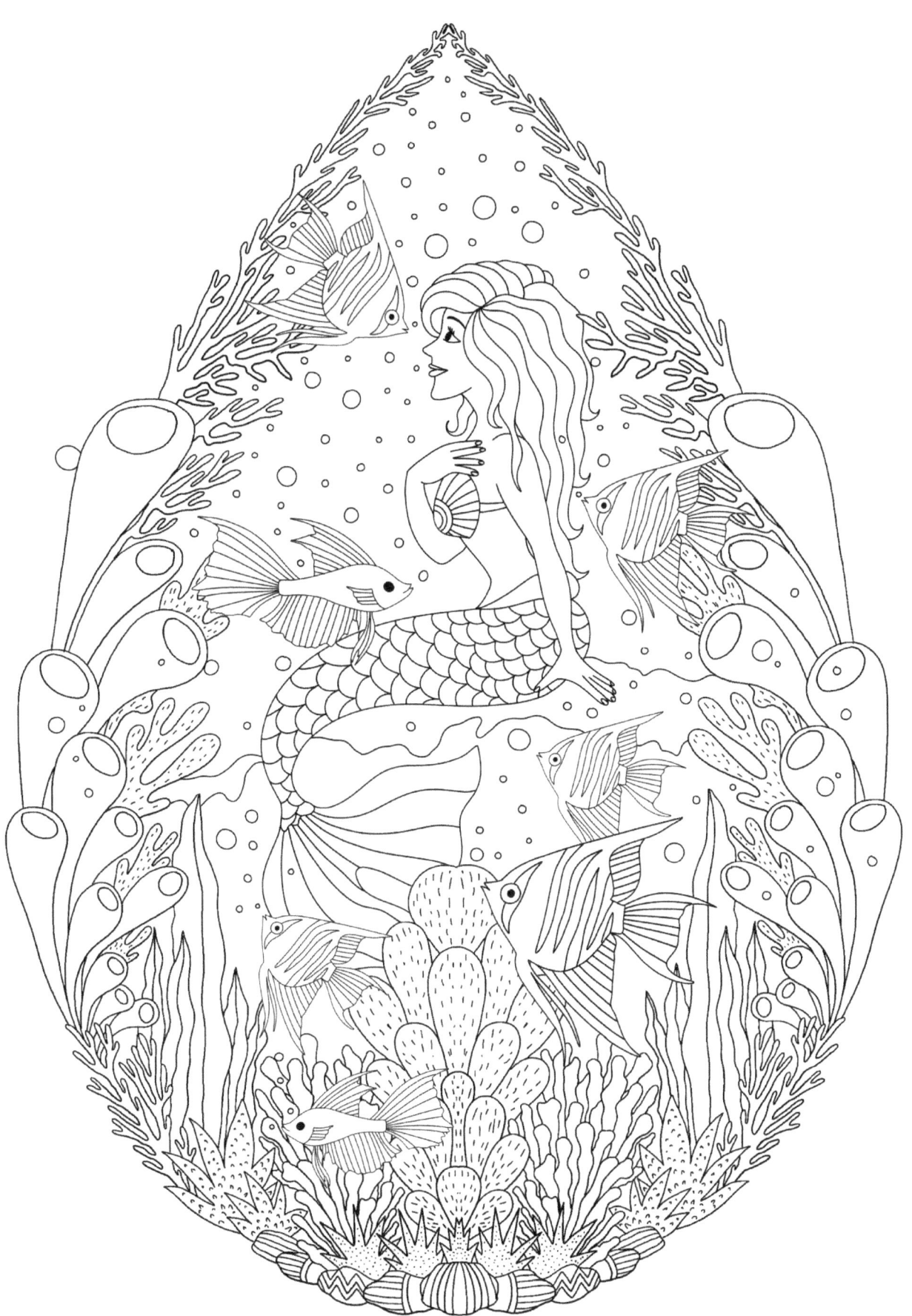

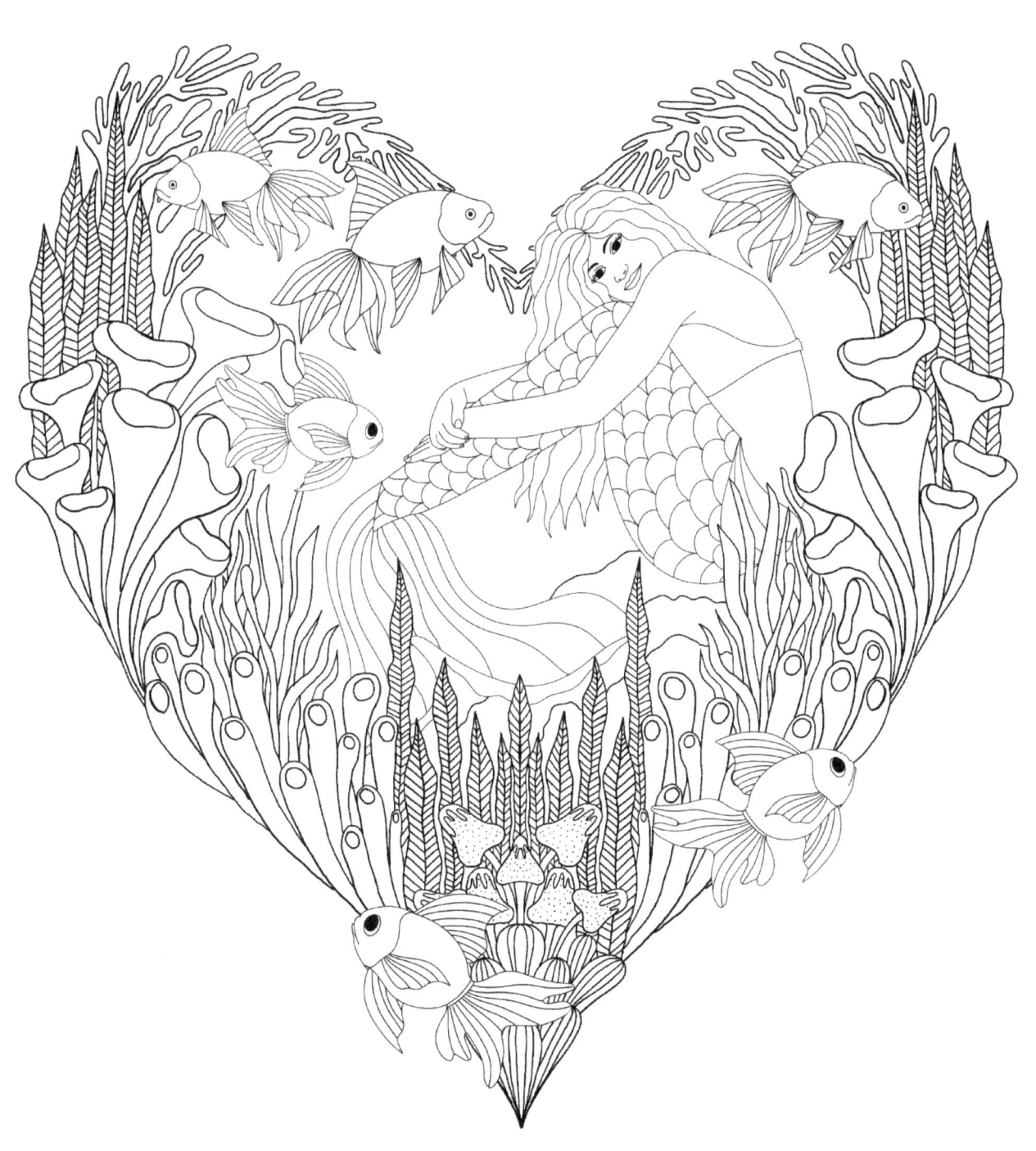

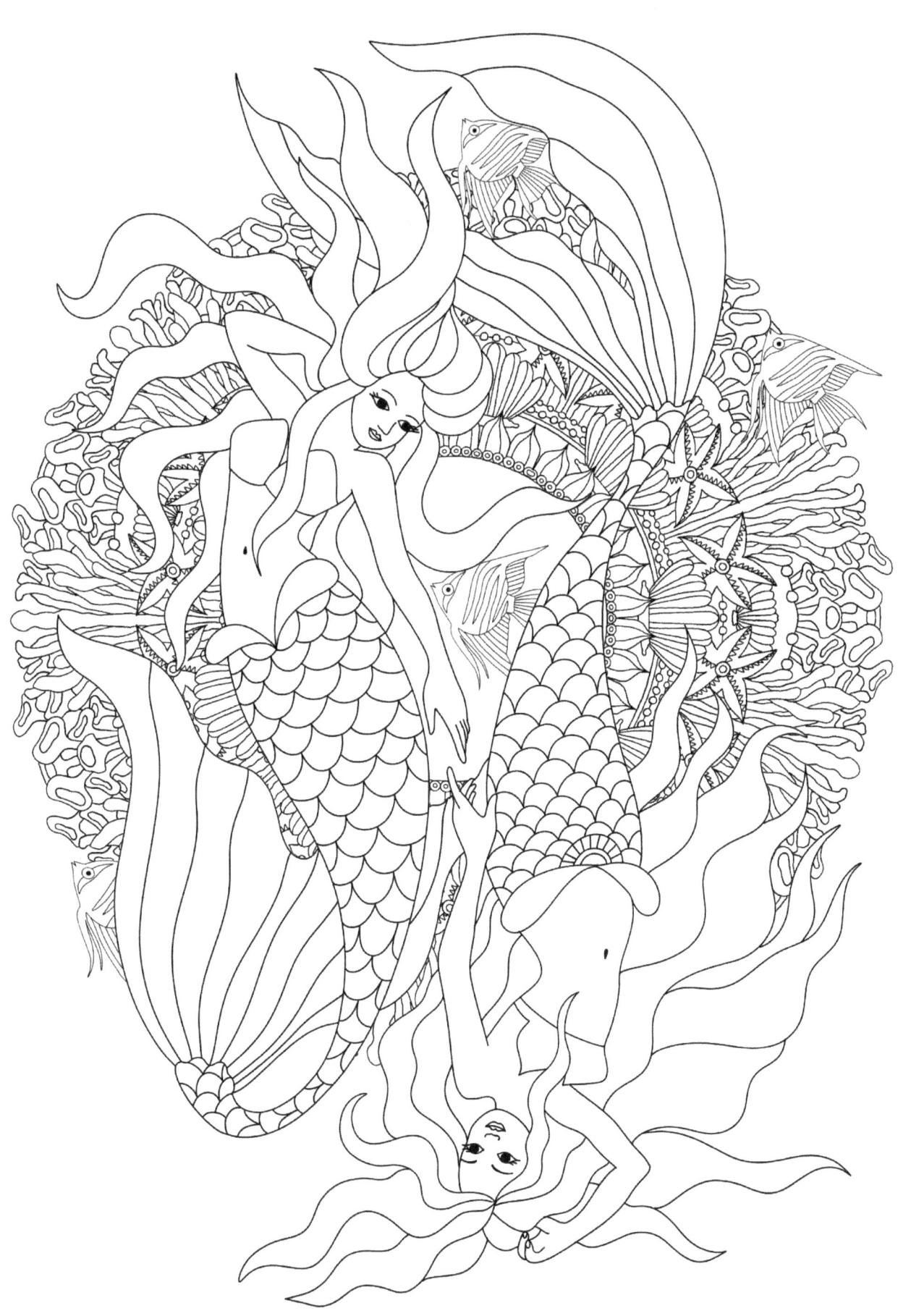

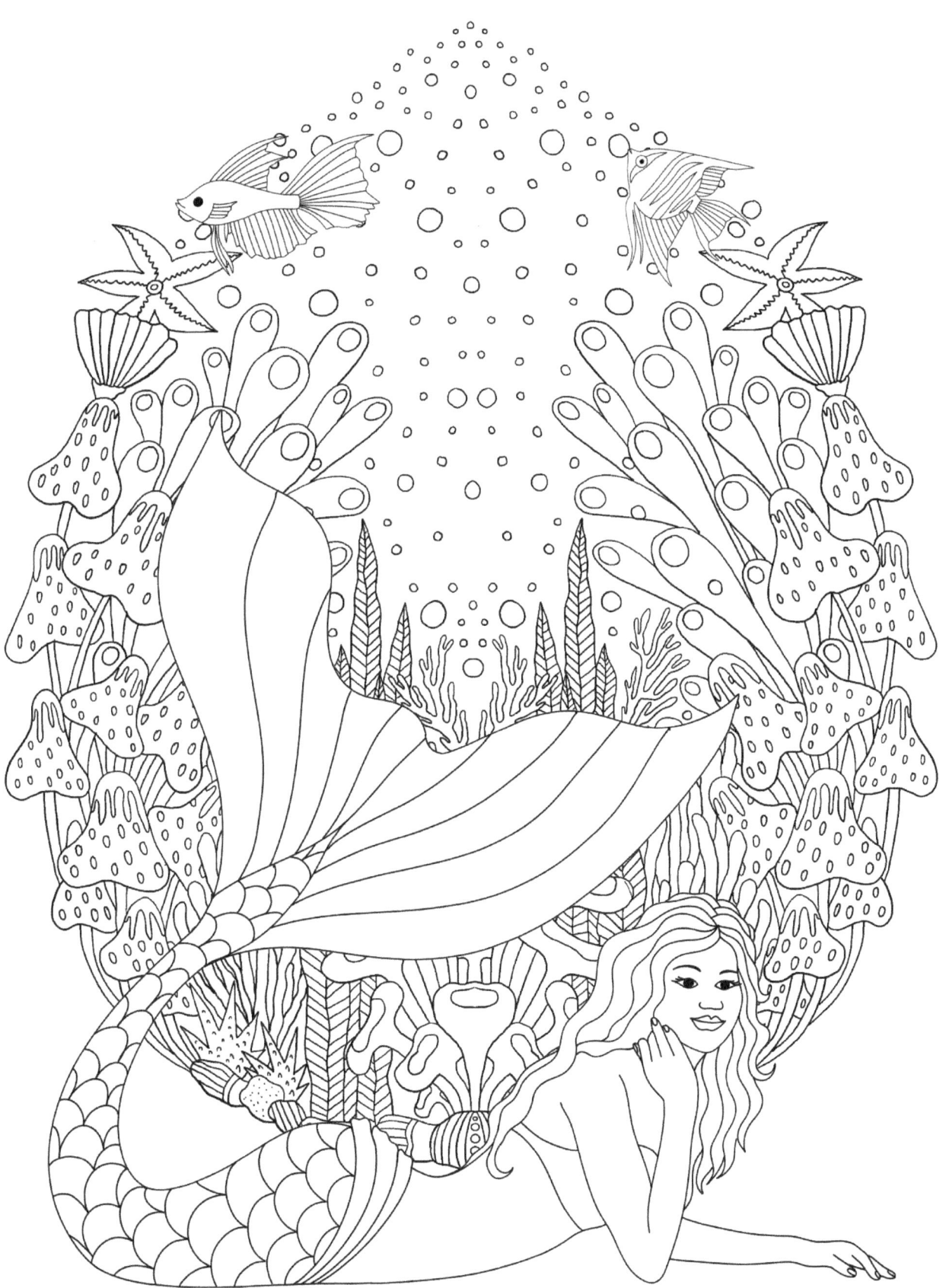

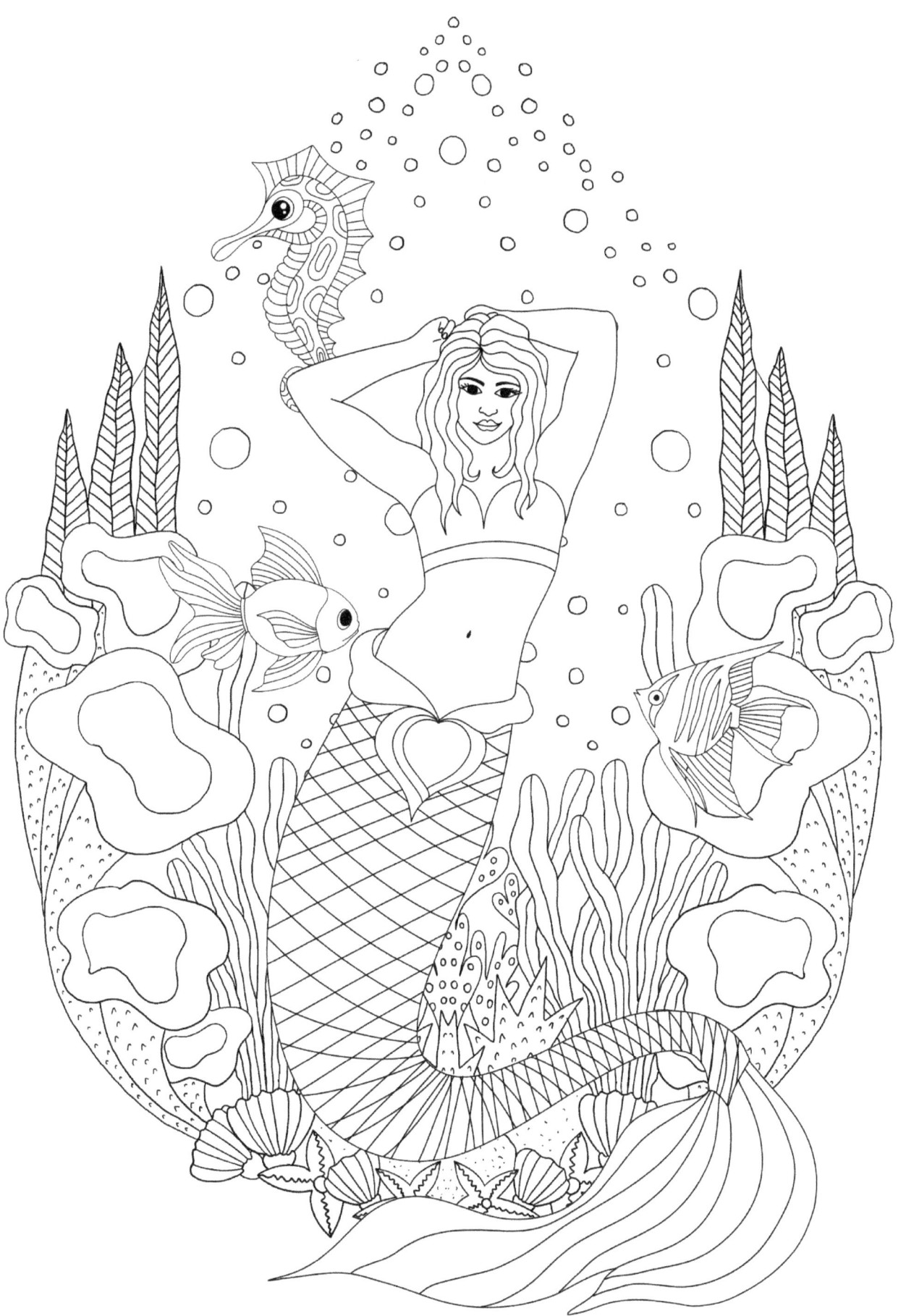

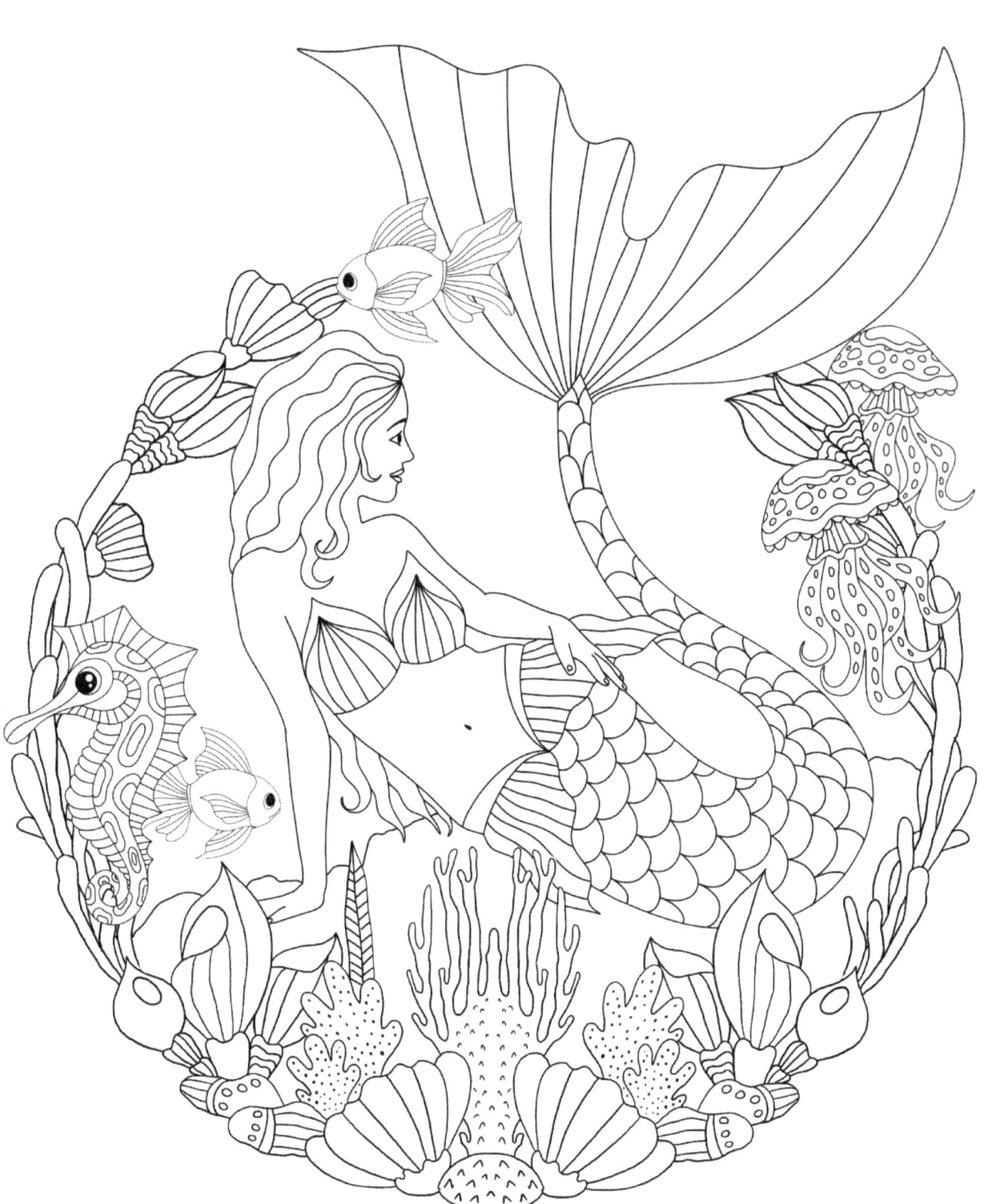

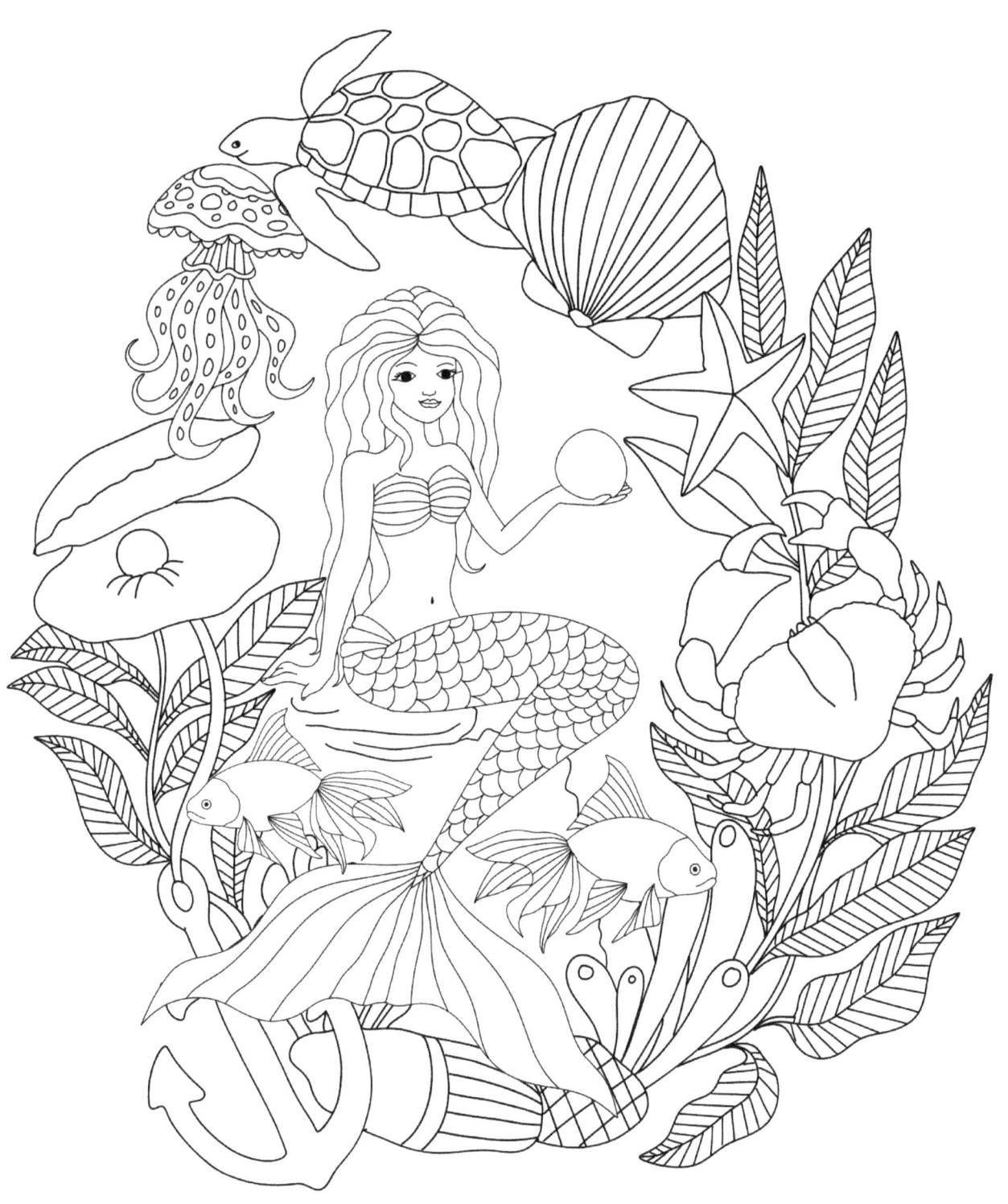

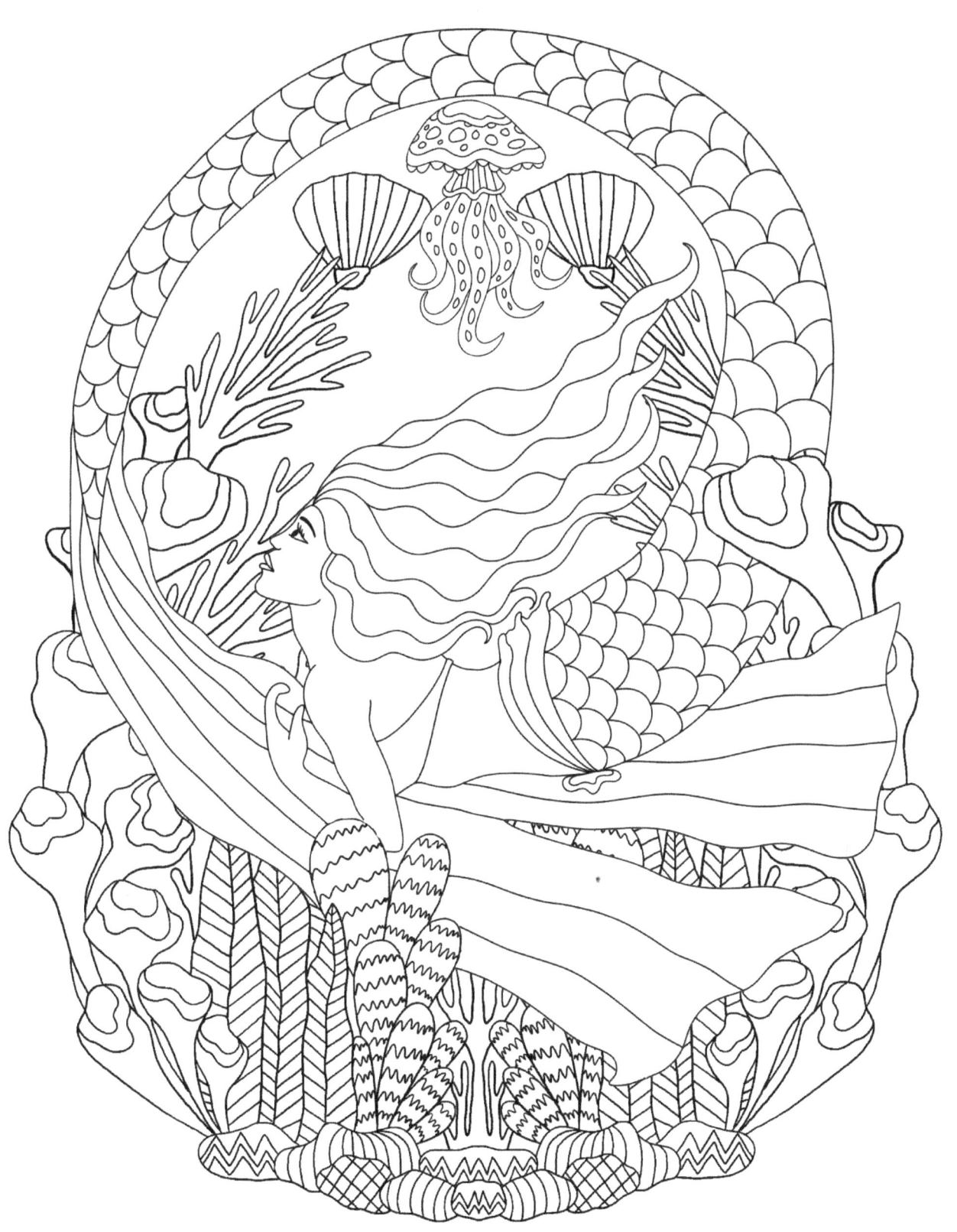

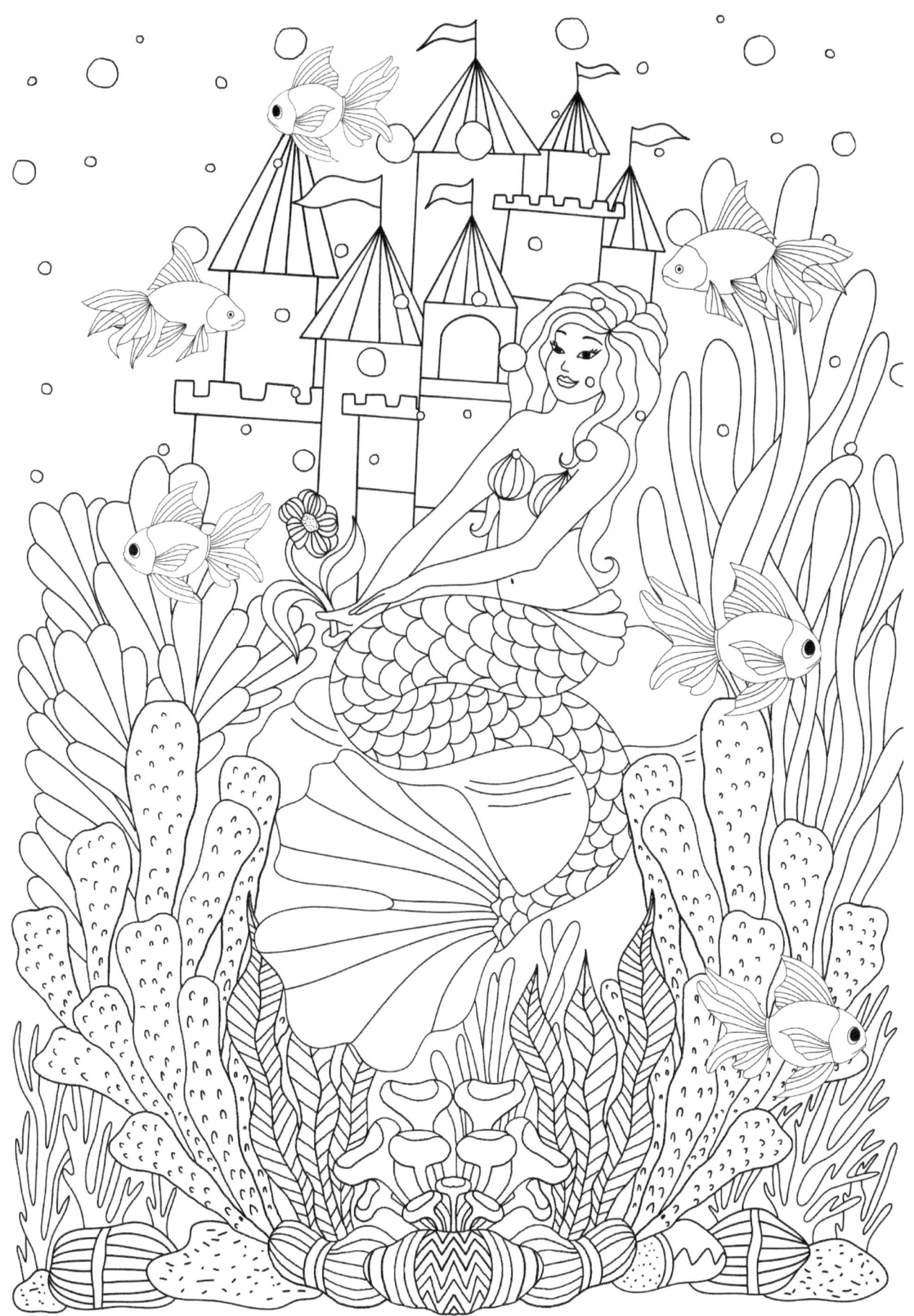

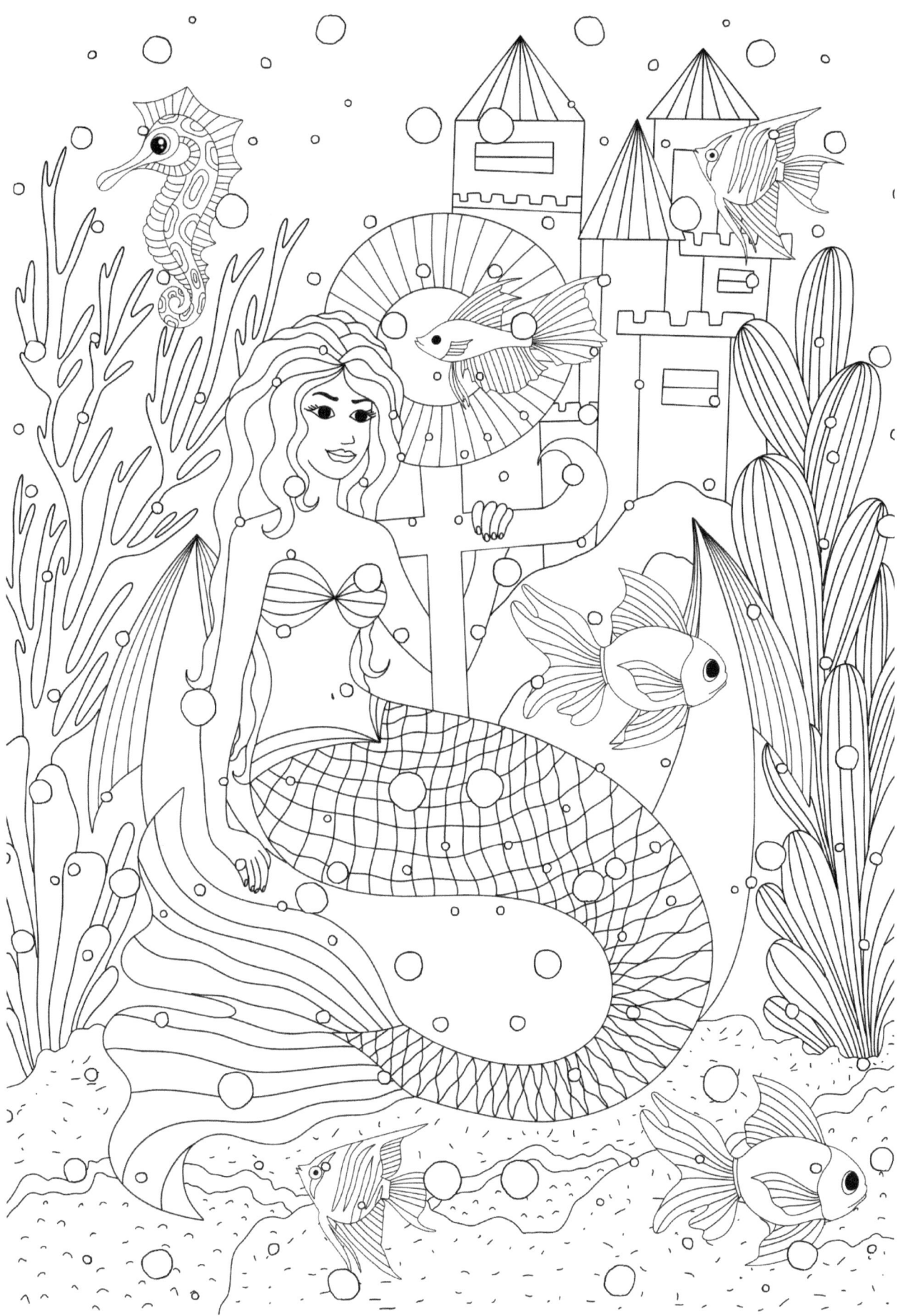

OTHER BOOKS BY PAUL SHORE

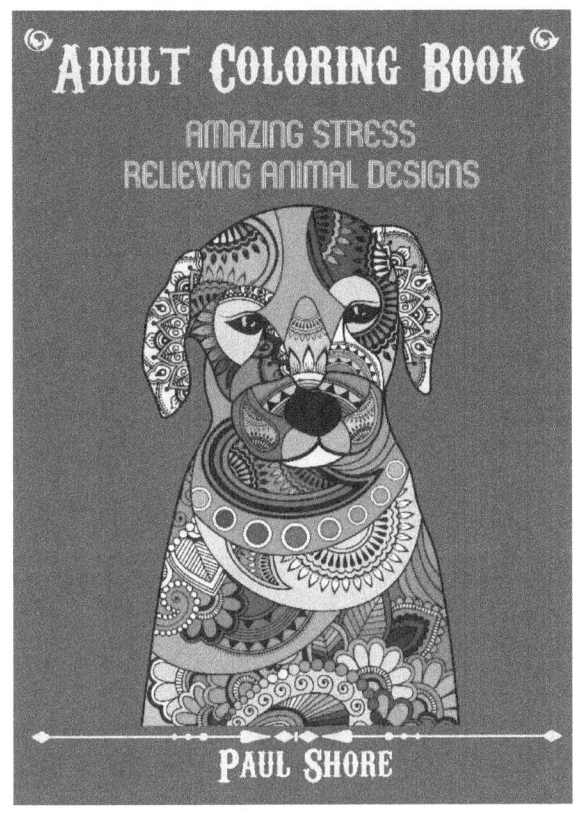

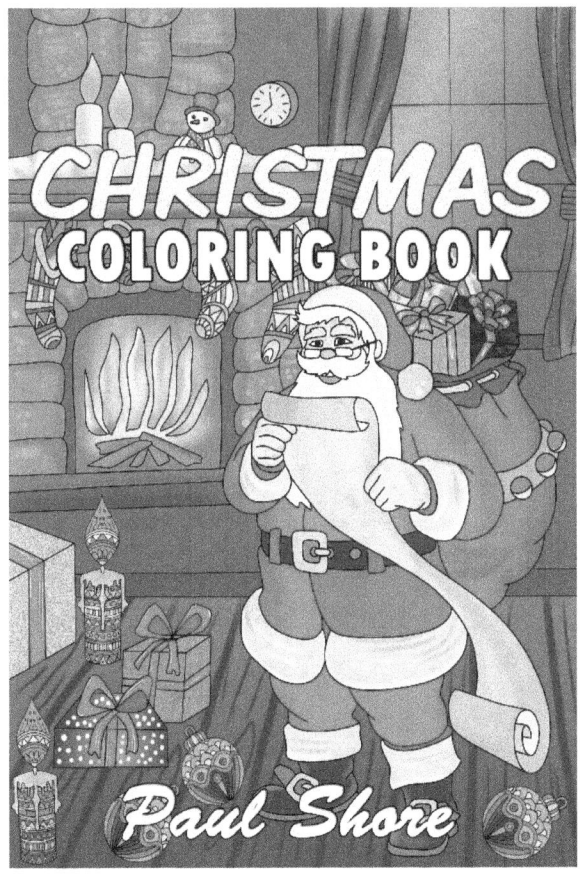

Thanks for purchasing a copy of our book. For a free copy of the electronic version as promised, please visit https://mailchi.mp/ce0ab0a7a758/mermaidcoloringbook to download a free electronic copy from the file section of the group.

As you enjoy your copy of this Mermaid Coloring Book, do share, with other community members, your creative paintings on the dedicated group.

Subscribe to our mailing list for a free copy of 10 premium adult pages that you can download right now and color away.

Follow us on our various social media pages for news and promotions:

   fb.com/adultcoloringbookbyPS

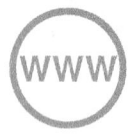   https://www.paulshorebooks.com

amazon.com/author/pshore

*If you enjoyed this book,
And had fun coloring the pages,
Why not then go online to write a sweet review!*

Thank you!

www.ingramcontent.com/pod-product-compliance
Lightning Source LLC
Chambersburg PA
CBHW062337220526
45469CB00008B/2752